Rebuilding the Foundations

by Paul Pavao

Publication date: October 1, 2021

ISBN

    Paperback: 978-1-7341060-1-5

    Digital Online: 978-1-7341060-2-2

Contact information:

    email: paul@christian-history.org

The PDF of this book may be downloaded at:
https://www.RebuildingTheFoundations.org/rebuilding-the-foundations.html

Copyright

Copyright 2018-2021 by Paul Pavao. Permission is hereby given to copy and distribute *Rebuilding the Foundations* in whole or in part, but not to change it nor to charge for it. All distribution of these words must be free. You may also cite this book extensively in your own work if proper attribution is given. The Kindle version of *Rebuilding the Foundations* is free as well.

Scripture Quotes

All Scripture quotations are from the World English Bible (WEB), a public domain translation. I made two changes regularly. I used "church" in the place of the WEB's "assembly" because people are more used to it. I used "the Lord" rather than the WEB's "Yahweh" because that is what the apostles did when they wrote in Greek.

Early Christian Quotes

Quotes from the early Christian writings (early church fathers) can be read in context at http://www.earlychristianwritings.com and https://www.ccel.org/fathers

Church or church

Throughout this book, I capitalize "Church" when I mean the universal Church or a section of the universal Church. I use "church" when discussing the local church.

Definition of Evangelical

This book is written with evangelicals in mind. There is no official definition of "evangelical." For my purposes, an evangelical is someone who believes ...

- being born again is an experience rather than the automatic consequence of baptism.
- the Bible is inspired by God.
- we are saved by faith in Jesus Christ.
- we need to preach the Gospel to the whole world.

This is a loose definition, but I mean for it to be. Among evangelical churches I would include Baptists, Methodists, Presbyterians, Lutherans, Reformed, Pentecostals, and similar denominations, especially those that trace their origin back to the Protestant Reformation. Most of these would welcome the designation "evangelical." I must exclude the "high church" Protestant denominations such as the Episcopalians and Anglicans because, honestly, I do not know enough about them.

Table of Contents

Rebuilding the Foundations i
   Copyright i
   Scripture Quotes ii
   Early Christian Quotes.. ii
   Church or church ii
   Definition of Evangelical ii
Table of Contents iii
Acknowledgments v
Introduction: The Need to Rebuild vii
1. Bulldozing the Old Foundations............................. 1
   Why Refute a Doctrine Most People Don't Believe? .. 3
   Rebuilding The Final Judgment of God 5
   Rebuilding Sacrifice and Mercy 10
   Aphesis 14
   Aphesis in the Septuagint 15
2. Building on the Right Rock.................................... 19
   More Reasons to Build on the Right Rock 26
3. God's Firm Foundation 31
   The Foundation of God 35
4. Rescuing Good Works 37
   The Purpose of the Scriptures 37
   The Purpose of the Atonement and Grace 38
   The Purpose of the New Birth 39
   The Purpose of Walking by and Sowing to the Spirit 40
   The Purpose of Assembling the Church 42
5. The Mercy of God 44
   Addictions 47

Whom Will God Not Charge with Sin?	48
Walking in the Light	50
6. Which Good Works?	55
Evangelism Is Not the Only Good Work	55
What Good Works Are	64
7. Rebuilding the Atonement	68
The "Favor" of Eternal Life	73
Old Testament Sacrifices	78
Ephesians 1:7 & Colossians 1:14	83
8. Salvation by Faith Alone and Other Objections	86
Salvation by Faith Alone	86
The Writings of the Apostle John	92
1 John 3:9	95
1 John 2:19: "They Were Never of Us"	99
1 Corinthians 3:15: Saved, But As Through Fire	105
Do Not Be Deceived	106
9. The "Do Not Be Deceived" Passages	108
10. Living Out God's Firm Foundation Today	111
Be Delivered from Disputing!	111
Other Calls to Action	114
Walk in the Light	115
The Church	116
Finding a Church	117
Disciple-Making Movements	122
Bibliography	125
Paul Pavao and Greatest Stories Ever Told®	131

Acknowledgments

God made my personality and guided the circumstances of my life to mold me to write this book. So, first, glory be to the Most High!

Thank you, Marlene Hidalgo, for convincing me this book was worth writing.

Thank you, Lorie Pavao. I cannot imagine living without you, much less writing this book. This book is infused with your love, hope, encouragement, and your fierce disciple's heart.

Thank you to all my friends, acquaintances, and enemies. You have helped shape both this book and me. You have taught me how to argue and how to communicate with the written word. I am certain I am not selfless, unbiased, nor dispassionate in my theology and writing, but I am much more so because of you.

Thank you to all of you who are and have been part of Rose Creek Village. You taught me to be courageous in my relationships, to be vulnerable, that weakness is universal among humans, and that God miraculously maintains and restores relationships. Thank you also for teaching me that unity in theology is a distant second to preserving the unity of the Holy Spirit.

Thank you, David Taylor, for allowing me to be myself when you had the power to prevent it. Thank you for allowing me to follow the Holy Spirit freely when you had authority to get in the way.

Thank you, Dassi Pavao, for making sacrifices to help me create the cover and for editing all my books. I cannot express how glad I am that you and Noah chose one another.

Thank you to the doctors, nurses, and staff of the Vanderbilt Cancer Clinic. I am only alive to write this book because of your knowledge, skill, faith, and the hopeful and happy environment you provided. I cannot possibly mention you all by name. I can mention Dr. Ratliff, of Boston-Baskin Cancer Foundation at the time, my only Memphis oncologist. Thank you for your confidence when side effects were worst. Your confidence was so helpful that only God could have provided you.

I could write a book about how many people I need to thank and how much I need to thank them. There are just too many names that belong on this page to list them all.

Introduction: The Need to Rebuild

The purpose of this book is to rescue the Bible from a paradigm—a view of God, Christianity, and salvation—that is riddled with errors from top to bottom. It has so many myths, non-scriptural taboos, and added traditions that there is no repairing it; it must be rebuilt from the foundation up.

This paradigm is common to evangelical denominations, and most certainly those that label themselves fundamentalists. It is held by millions of American Christians and permeates both hymn books and contemporary Christian music. It is widely accepted and unquestioned among those who hold it, but it is nonetheless obviously unscriptural.

I want to emphasize, as I will throughout the book, that the evangelical paradigm has something very important right: We need Jesus' grace, God's love, and the fellowship of the Holy Spirit to live a life marked by good works (2 Cor. 13:14; Jn. 15:5; Rom. 8:2-4; Gal. 6:7-9).

I pray that is where you are starting *before* you read this book. If you do not have the Holy Spirit, you will not be able to live out the teachings in this book. Therefore, I will cover the Good News through which you may receive the Holy Spirit early in the book. For those with the Holy Spirit, this book can empower you. Believing the right things about your salvation will help you to "be transformed by the renewing of your mind, so that you may prove what is the good, well-pleasing, and perfect will of God."

The teachings in this book were once the foundational teachings of all Christians.[1] It seems obvious to me that the original teachings of the church, held by all the apostolic churches in unity, are much more trustworthy than doctrines argued over by multiple denominations and churches two thousand years after Jesus. Nonetheless, I am not going to teach them from the writings

---

[1] I have spent thirty years and hundreds of hours reading the teachings of the earliest Christians in books you can now read online for free at http://www.earlychristianwritings.com and https://www.CCEL.org/fathers. I have many articles on early Christianity at https://www.christian-history.org.

of the early churches, but from the Bible, which we all agree is the most authoritative source for Christian teaching.

I am zealous for the teachings in the book. I know, though, that one of the most important things I can do is eagerly "keep the unity of the Spirit in the bond of peace" (Eph. 4:3). Thirty years ago, I was guilty of using accurate teaching to divide born-again saints with whom I should have preserved unity of Spirit. Today, as I write this introduction, I would rather never speak nor write again than divide the ones Jesus calls his own.

Of course, I want you to read this book and understand the Scriptures properly. More importantly, I want you to feel compelled to *obey* the Scriptures. Jesus is the "author of eternal salvation" to those who obey him (Heb. 5:9). It will do you no good to hear my teachings, nor those from Jesus, if you do not obey them (Matt. 7:24-27).

Finally, I want to plead with you not to use the teachings in my book to divide the saints, but to build yourself up in faith so you can build up others. This will take wisdom, but Jesus has become wisdom from God for us (1 Cor. 1:30), God has promised wisdom to those who ask (James 1:5), and with some practice, you will be able to apply wisdom in every aspect of your life (Heb. 5:14).

1. Bulldozing the Old Foundations

In this book, I am going to establish, explain, and build on "God's firm foundation" (2 Tim. 2:19). But just as Jeremiah had to uproot, tear down, destroy, and overthrow before he could build and plant (Jer. 1:10), so I must remove the old foundation before I rebuild the biblical one. The old foundation, built with tradition rather than Scripture, is far too weak to hold the solid and ancient oaks of scriptural truth.

What I did not know when I began is that there is one solidly entrenched cornerstone holding all that tradition together, making it extremely difficult to remove. It is, in fact, not a stone, but a vine, at least half a millennium old, with thick twisted roots and tendrils wrapped around every crumbling piece of the old foundation.

That vine is horrifying to the mind, repulsive to the conscience, and directly contradicts dozens of Bible passages, yet it has somehow become the heart of evangelical theology. That vine is the strange idea that ...

God cannot forgive sin without a blood sacrifice!

I am going to guess that you did not gasp when you read that line. It has no pop. Let us try its firstfruit instead:

Even the smallest sin deserves eternal damnation.

That has a little more pop. In this Information Age, this horrific idea draws the shock it deserves. In fact, Ligonier Ministries reports that a 2017 survey showed that 61% of participants strongly disagreed with the statement.[2] I was thrilled, but Ligonier's response will help you understand how deeply rooted this doctrine is. They wrote:

---

[2] The State of Theology, 2017, "The State of Theology," statement no. 12; In 2020, the page was changed to say, "Itis because of God's holiness that we understand how significant sin is." In 2021, they removed the question from the page.

> If [God] is perfectly holy and just, he cannot let sin go unpunished. But God is no longer holy—in the minds of six out of ten Americans.[3]

This statement from Ligonier Ministries has to be among the worst accusations ever made against God. Can it possibly be "holy and just," under any circumstances, to eternally condemn—in burning fire, no less—a 10-year-old whose only sin was to cheat on a fourth-grade test? Detention for a week, maybe, or even two weeks, and a paddle on the butt from dad, but eternal torture? No!

That question is no longer on Ligonier's "State of Theology" page, but they do have a blog post verifying that I did not make up the question. Their October 12, 2016, blog post discusses the 2016 survey. It reads:

> Of the 47 statements included in The State of Theology study for 2016, undertaken in partnership with LifeWay Research, the responses to one statement stood out. Most of the responses tended to even out over the spectrum. Each statement tended to garner slight majorities. ... But not statement 17, "Even the smallest sin deserves eternal damnation." This one sparked a reaction. ... 61% strongly disagree. Another 12% disagree somewhat and 7% are not sure. That leaves only 21% agreeing with this statement.[4]

Stephen Nichols, the author of the blog post, was not afraid to add:

> We need to interpret this data. Eight out of ten Americans have an incorrect view of sin. As an implication, we could say that eight out of ten Americans do not know the biblical God.[5]

This book is written to prove to you beyond a shadow of a doubt that the "biblical" God is nothing like Ligonier's caricature of him. Instead, the biblical God says, "Have I any pleasure in the death of the wicked ... and not rather that he should return from his way, and live?" (Ezek. 18:23). The biblical God is:

---

[3] The State of Theology, 2017, "The State of Theology"
[4] Nichols, 2016, "The State of Theology," par. 1-2
[5] Nichols, 2016, "The State of Theology," par. 2

> ... a merciful and gracious God, slow to anger, and abundant in loving kindness and truth, keeping loving kindness for thousands, forgiving iniquity and disobedience and sin; and who will by no means clear the guilty. (Ex. 34:6-7)

This is a radically different picture of God than the one Ligonier Ministries suggests! Thank God only 21% of Americans agree with Ligonier!

Why Refute a Doctrine Most People Don't Believe?

If 80% of American disagree with this doctrine, then why am I bothering to refute it?

The purpose of this book is not refutation. It is rebuilding the original foundation that has been broken to pieces by the vine I described earlier, "a vine, at least half a millennium old, with thick twisted roots and tendrils wrapped around every crumbling piece of the old foundation."

It is impossible to rebuild the old foundation without removing the vine that has roots so thick that ancient teachings, once held by "the Church ... scattered through the whole world ... in Germany... in Spain ... in Gaul ... in the East ... in Egypt ... in Libya ... [and] in the central regions in the world"[6] are now largely forgotten.

Though the specific teaching that the smallest sin deserves eternal damnation is so distasteful that it is falling out of favor with American Christians, it has been around for centuries, affecting everything we believe. Anyone who has tried to remove a vine knows what a great multitude of tightly wound tendrils, firmly attached stems, and deep roots they have.

Ligonier Ministries is an overtly Calvinist ministry. The idea they are espousing, that even the smallest sin deserves eternal damnation, is a central tenet of Calvinism. In a 1963 book published by the Presbyterian & Reformed Publishing Company, David Steele and Curtis Thomas wrote this about Calvinist doctrines:

> If, in your investigation, you probe into the history and influence of Calvinism, you will discover that its doctrines have

---

[6] Irenaeus, c. 185, *Against Heresies*, Bk. I, ch. 10, par. 2

been incorporated into the majority of the great creeds of the Protestant churches.[7]

McClintock and Strong's add:

> Calvinism has formed the doctrinal basis of the Presbyterian Church, the Reformed Church, the Episcopal Church of America, and in the main the Baptist and Congregationalist Churches, which include the United Church of Christ. Most aspects of Calvinistic ideology are found in the Nazarene Church, the Evangelical Lutheran Church, and almost all so called "Evangelical" churches.[8]

A doctrine so deeply entrenched that it was incorporated into "the majority of the great creeds of the Protestant churches" must leave a mark. I remember being taught as a young Christian that "God ... doesn't want to punish us," but because he is just, "he must punish us."[9] I learned this in an evangelism program published by a Presbyterian church and taught to me in an Assemblies of God church.[10] A few years later I would be taught the same thing by the Southern Baptist's *Continuing Witness Training*. I remember wondering what force or being could require God to punish us when he wanted to forgive us.

The evangelism program I was taught was "Evangelism Explosion" from a book written by Dr. D. James Kennedy in 1970. *Evangelism Explosion* has been translated into over 70 languages and used all over the world.[11] This idea that God cannot show mercy because his justice forces him to punish sin is the direct product of the Calvinist teaching that even the smallest sin deserves eternal damnation.

Don't get me wrong. I am thrilled that Jesus' name is being proclaimed all over the world. I have been several places in the world myself to help others preach the Gospel. Paul said he was

---

[7] Steele & Thomas, 1963, *The Five Points of Calvinism*, p. 61; cited by Osburn, 2019, "Calvinism"

[8] McClintock & Strong, 1891, Cyclopaedia Biblical Theological Ecclesiastical Literature, Vol. II; cited by Osburn, 2019, "Calvinism"

[9] ABC Memphis, 2021, "Evangelism Explosion Outline"

[10] Kennedy, 1970, *Evangelism Explosion*

[11] Evangelism Explosion International, 2018, "History"

glad when the name of Jesus was preached, even for the wrong reasons, and so am I. Nonetheless, it is surely better to preach Jesus biblically, the way the apostles preached him, rather than the way later traditions preach him.

Nowhere does the Bible teach that the smallest sin deserves eternal condemnation. Instead, it teaches that the God who judges us will be our loving Father who has never desired the death of the wicked, but their repentance (Ezek. 18:23).

With that, let's begin ripping that vine all the way out of the ground and grinding its roots to powder.

Rebuilding The Final Judgment of God

There is one passage that evangelicals use, the only one that can be used, to defend the idea that even the smallest sins must be punished, though it says nothing at all about eternal damnation, nor anything about the final judgment.

The passage is in James 2 and talks about showing favoritism to one another, yet Calvinists have made it the gold standard for God's final judgment. It reads:

> But if you show favoritism, you sin and are convicted by the law as lawbreakers. For whoever keeps the whole law and yet stumbles at just one point is guilty of breaking all of it. For he who said, "You shall not commit adultery," also said, "You shall not murder." If you do not commit adultery but do commit murder, you have become a lawbreaker. (James 2:8-11)

This passage warns us not to favor one person over another because we are all lawbreakers, having violated God's law in one way or another. It does *not* say that God will judge us for breaking one small point of the law; it says we should not judge *one another* because we are all lawbreakers.

James 2:8-11 teaches that any violation of the law makes you a lawbreaker. It does *not* say all lawbreakers deserve eternal damnation. In fact, it says nothing at all about eternal damnation, nor who deserves it.

There are passages that talk about what violators of the law deserve. A very good one is the story of the adulterous woman (John 8:3-11). Jesus was teaching a small crowd near the temple.

The scribes and Pharisees broke into their gathering and stood a woman in front of him. They announced, "Teacher, we found this woman in adultery, in the very act."

I am sure the sarcasm dripped from their tongues as they unknowingly confronted their Creator and future Judge. "Now in our law, Moses commanded us to stone such women. What then do you say about her?"

Oddly, Jesus stooped down and wrote on the ground with his finger. I have heard several guesses as to what he was writing, my favorite being the name of the Pharisees' mistresses. My guess is that the hypocritical condemnation of this woman, the ignoring of the man that was with her, and the sneering tone of the arrogant Pharisees infuriated the Son of God, who was a man tempted in every way we are (Heb. 4:15). Writing on the ground, whatever he wrote, may have given him time to refrain from 'un-creating' them with a thought, dissolving their miserable hides into sub-atomic particles.

Whatever the reason, he wrote long enough to simply state, in so many words, "All of you who have not broken the law, you have the right to throw a stone at her."

James 2:10 is right. We are all lawbreakers. Even the Pharisees, when Jesus called them on it, could not deny it.

We also find out, through Jesus, just what God thinks we lawbreakers deserve: a second chance. Or maybe it was a third chance ... or a fourth ... or a forty-fourth ... or maybe the four-hundred-and-ninetieth (70 times 7; Matt. 18:22). Jesus told her, "Woman, where are your accusers? Did no one condemn you? ... Neither do I condemn you. Go your way. From now on, sin no more" (Jn. 8:10-11).

Here we have an actual case of how Jesus, and thus God, looks at adultery. Like all other sins, he forgives, and he asks the sinner to stop sinning. The people who aroused God's wrath were the proud and hypocritical (Matt. 23).

Jesus gave us multiple examples of the way he, and thus his Father, judges. In his judgment, sinners need his physician-like skills to repent and become righteous (Luke 5:31-32). For example, Jesus called Zacchaeus, a tax collector, out of a tree to eat with him. Tax collectors were traitors in the eyes of their fellow Israelites. Those taxes went to the Roman Empire, which held Israel captive. Even worse, most overcharged their fellow Jews to pad their own pockets. Zacchaeus was probably one of them. After Jesus brought him to repentance, he said, "If I have wrongfully exacted anything of anyone, I restore four times as much."

According to Hebrews 1:3, Jesus is "the exact representation" of the Father's being. We can expect, then, that the Father judges like the Son, and that is exactly what we find. In fact, God argues vehemently, through Ezekiel and against Israel, that it is just to judge the very way Jesus judged the adulteress woman.

> "The soul who sins, he shall die: the son shall not bear the iniquity of the father, neither shall the father bear the iniquity of the son; the righteousness of the righteous shall be on him, and the wickedness of the wicked shall be on him. But if the wicked turn from all his sins that he has committed, and keep all my statutes, and do that which is lawful and right, he shall surely live, he shall not die. None of his transgressions that he has committed shall be remembered against him: in his righteousness that he has done he shall live. Have I any pleasure in the death of the wicked?" says the Lord God, "and not rather that he should return from his way, and live?
>
> "But when the righteous turns away from his righteousness, and commits iniquity, and does according to all the abominations that the wicked man does, shall he live? None of his righteous deeds that he has done shall be remembered: in his trespass that he has trespassed, and in his sin that he has sinned, in them shall he die.
>
> "Yet you say, 'The way of the Lord is not fair.' Hear now, house of Israel: Is my way not fair? Aren't your ways unfair? When the righteous man turns away from his righteousness, and commits iniquity, and dies therein; in his iniquity that he has done he shall die. Again, when the wicked man turns away from his wickedness that he has committed, and does that which is lawful and right, he shall save his soul alive. Because he considers and turns away from all his transgressions that he has committed, he shall surely live, he shall not die. Yet the house of Israel says, 'The way of the Lord

is not fair.' House of Israel, aren't my ways fair? Aren't your ways unfair?

"Therefore I will judge you, house of Israel, everyone according to his ways," says the Lord God. "Return, and turn yourselves from all your transgressions; so iniquity shall not be your ruin. Cast away from you all your transgressions, in which you have transgressed; and make yourself a new heart and a new spirit: for why will you die, house of Israel? For I have no pleasure in the death of him who dies," says the Lord God. "Therefore turn yourselves, and live." (Ezek. 18:20-32)

God put a lot of words into defending his idea of a just judgment. In fact, there are similar descriptions of how God deals with the lawless in Ezekiel 3:18-21 and 33:8-20. That form of judgment is exactly the form of judgment Jesus exercised. He commands the wicked to repent, and if they do, he forgets all the wickedness they have ever done. Their newfound righteousness will reap life for them.

It is apparent that the righteousness God demands is not sinless perfection. Both the Old Testament and the New Testament tell us that no one is without sin, not even the righteous or the born again (1 Kings 8:46; Jas. 3:2; 1 Jn. 1:8-10). Instead, under both the Old Testament and New Testament, there are those "whose sin the Lord will never count against them." (Ps. 32:2; Rom. 4:6-8).

Rather than sinless perfection being the only righteousness God accepts, there are people so righteous that God will not only reward them, but others as well!

"Son of man, if a country sins against me by being unfaithful and I stretch out my hand against it to cut off its food supply and send famine upon it and kill its people and their animals, even if these three men—Noah, Daniel and Job—were in it, they could save only themselves by their righteousness, declares the Sovereign Lord." (Ezek. 14:13-14)

Through Ezekiel, God listed three men who were righteous enough to have saved themselves from the judgment that came upon Judah. In fact, the implication is that under normal circumstances, they would not only have saved themselves but also the entire "country." Judah, though, had sinned so badly that God had allowed Babylon to destroy Jerusalem and the temple and take her people into captivity. He was not going to forgive them until the prophesied 70 years were fulfilled (Jer. 29:10), "even if these three men ... were in it." Nonetheless, God held these three men up as righteous enough to save themselves from judgment.

Noah, Daniel, and Job occasionally sinned. It is recorded that Job "darken[ed] counsel by words without knowledge" (Job 38:1). This is, in my estimation, a small sin, but the Calvinist god thinks the smallest sin deserves eternal damnation. The true God did not think Job deserved condemnation at all, but a strong rebuke followed by praise and restoration (Job 38-42). Job was righteous in God's eyes even though he sinned. We can be sure that Noah and Daniel sinned as well whether Noah's drunkenness (Gen. 9:20-21) qualifies as sin or not. Everyone sins. Even under the New Covenant, the Apostle John stated that anyone claiming to have no sin is a liar (1 Jn. 1:8). Nonetheless, God had the highest regard for the righteousness of Noah, Daniel, and Job.

In my mind, this brings up Lot. When God told Abraham that he was going to destroy Sodom and Gomorrah, Abraham was horrified. He knew that Lot lived there. He bargained with God until God agreed that if there were ten righteous people in Sodom, he would spare the city (Gen. 18:16-32).

As it so happened, there were not ten righteous in Sodom. God found only four but, in his mercy, he removed them from Sodom before he destroyed it (Gen. 19:1-17).

The point is, God would have spared an extremely wicked city for the sake of ten righteous people. He did not require sacrifice to spare the city, but righteousness. (We will cover sacrifices in the chapter on the atonement.)

We must remember, too, that Lot was not all that righteous. He "was tormented in his righteous soul" living in Sodom (2 Pet. 2:8), yet he was very slow to leave it. In fact, after the angels were forced to pull him out of the city, he asked to go to another nearby city that was also under God's judgment (Gen. 19:16-23). God spared the city because Lot was in it, but Lot left the city almost immediately (Gen. 19:30).

Note that Abraham appeals to God's status as Judge of all the earth as a reason not to destroy the righteous with the wicked. The Judge of all the earth does not think that anyone who commits one sin deserves eternal punishment. Instead, he thinks that there are people who honor him and try to obey him, that those obedient people deserve to be called righteous, and that he should avoid punishing the wicked if that would cause the righteous to be punished as well.

This is a much different description of God than the Calvinist one.

This is a good spot to dismiss another myth. We evangelicals regularly quote Isaiah 64:6 and interpret it to mean that even when we do good, our righteousness is as filthy as menstrual rags. This is not the case. Isaiah 64:6 was a specific lament by Isaiah regarding Israel during a specific period. The passage is regularly quoted by us, but it was never quoted by Jesus or the apostles. Indeed, it is apparent that the righteousness of Noah, Daniel, and Job was not considered filthy in any way by God.

It is not just Noah, Daniel, and Job whom God regarded as righteous. God tells us through Ezekiel that anyone who turns from their wickedness and begins to do righteousness will live because of their righteousness. Their wickedness will never be brought up to them! (Ezek. 18:22). I remind you again that this is not sinless righteousness we are talking about because there is no one who does not sin (James 3:2; 1 John 1:7-2:2), not even Job, Noah, and Daniel.

Rebuilding Sacrifice and Mercy

You may remember that the first Calvinist doctrine I brought up was *God cannot forgive sin without sacrifice*. John Calvin did not invent this doctrine. St. Anselm, an eleventh century Roman Catholic planted the seeds of the idea, and Thomas Aquinas, the famed thirteenth-century theologian, also a Roman Catholic, brought it to full bloom. Nonetheless, it was Calvin and his teachings that carried the idea "into the majority of the great creeds of the Protestant churches."[12]

The Bible does not teach that God cannot forgive sin without sacrifice, even though Hebrews 9:22 seems to teach that:

> According to the law, nearly everything is cleansed with blood, and apart from shedding of blood there is no remission.

Most people understand "remission" to mean forgiveness. Most modern translations, such as the NIV and NASB, have "forgiveness" in Hebrews 9:22 rather than "remission."

If "remission" means forgiveness, then Hebrews 9:22 denies everything I have written in this book. If "remission" means forgiveness, then Hebrews 9:22 teaches that God cannot forgive sin unless blood is shed. Worse, if "remission" means forgiveness, then God's character is worse than yours or mine because you and I forgive our children's sins without shedding the blood of animals or humans. In fact, if we were to shed blood every time one of our children disobeyed, we would wind up in jail.

Not only that, but if God cannot forgive sin without the shedding of blood, then David knew neither God nor the Law of Moses. After sinning with Bathsheba, he wrote:

> For you don't delight in sacrifice, or else I would give it. You have no pleasure in burnt offering. The sacrifices of God are a broken spirit. O God, you will not despise a broken and contrite heart. (Ps. 51:16-17)

God himself did not know about this requirement. He told the wayward kingdom of Judah:

> The Lord of Armies, the God of Israel says: "Add your burnt offerings to your sacrifices and eat meat. For I didn't speak to your fathers or command them in the day that I brought them out of the land of Egypt concerning burnt offerings or sacrifices; but this thing I commanded them, saying, 'Listen to my voice, and I will be your God, and you shall be my people.

---

[12] McClintock & Strong, 1891, Cyclopaedia Biblical Theological Ecclesiastical Literature, Vol. II; cited by Osburn, 2019, "Calvinism"

Walk in all the way that I command you, that it may be well with you.'" (Jer. 7:21-23).

The first line of that passage is sarcasm. With many of Israel's sacrifices, only the inedible parts were burned. The offerer and the priests got to eat all or most of the sacrifice (e.g., Lev. 7:11-18). This was not true of burnt offerings. Even the meat was to be offered in a burnt offering (Lev. 1:1-9). God is telling Israel to go ahead and ignore the Law of Moses and eat their burnt offerings. They were surely already doing this, and God sarcastically tells them to continue because he did not care about their offerings; he cared about, and still cares about, obedience. As Samuel said to Saul:

> Samuel said, "Has the Lord as great delight in burnt offerings and sacrifices, as in obeying the Lord's voice? Behold, to obey is better than sacrifice, and to listen than the fat of rams." (1 Sam. 15:22)

God said much the same thing to all of Israel through Isaiah as he said to Judah through Jeremiah:

> "What are the multitude of your sacrifices to me?" says the Lord. "I have had enough of the burnt offerings of rams and the fat of fed animals. I don't delight in the blood of bulls, or of lambs, or of male goats. When you come to appear before me, who has required this at your hand, to trample my courts? Bring no more vain offerings. Incense is an abomination to me. New moons, Sabbaths, and convocations: I can't stand evil assemblies. My soul hates your New Moons and your appointed feasts. They are a burden to me. I am weary of bearing them. When you spread out your hands, I will hide my eyes from you. Yes, when you make many prayers, I will not hear. Your hands are full of blood." (Isa. 1:11-15)

Because of Israel's behavior, God hated their sacrifices and feasts. Then he tells them what he really wants from them:

> Wash yourselves. Make yourself clean. Put away the evil of your doings from before my eyes. Cease to do evil. Learn to do well. Seek justice. Relieve the oppressed. Defend the fatherless. Plead for the widow. (Isa. 1:16-17)

If they would do that, then:

> Come now, and let's reason together," says the Lord: "Though your sins are as scarlet, they shall be white as snow. Though they be red like crimson, they shall be as wool. (Isa. 1:18)

Clearly, God can and did forgive sin without blood sacrifice. In fact, you may have noticed that God did not want sacrifice from his people at all while they were living in sin. The Law of Moses does call for sacrifices, and God does call those sacrifices a sweet savor (e.g., Ex. 29:18), but it is apparent that he only wants them from an obedient Israel. It would be fair, then, to say that it is not the sacrifice that purifies the person, but the pure heart of the offerer that purifies the sacrifice.

God has always forgiven sin without sacrifice. He has always wanted his people to do good and has never required sinlessness. God appeared in bodily form to Moses and announced:

> The Lord! The Lord, a merciful and gracious God, slow to anger, and abundant in loving kindness and truth, keeping loving kindness for thousands, forgiving iniquity and disobedience and sin; and who will by no means clear the guilty, visiting the iniquity of the fathers on the children, and on the children's children, on the third and on the fourth generation. (Ex. 34:6-7)

God's foremost attribute, after love, is mercy. It never stops, and it is new every morning (Lam. 3:22). That verse is in the Old Testament, and it was written by Jeremiah while Judah was in captivity in Babylon. Even when the Jews were so evil for so long that God destroyed their temple and sent them into captivity, they knew God's mercy never ends! Jonah knew this so well that he refused to prophesy to Nineveh because he knew God would show them mercy too! (Jonah 4:2).

Jesus did not die so that God would show us mercy at the final judgment! He was already going to show mercy to the righteous at the final judgment. It is only the guilty he condemns (Ex. 34:7).

So why then, does Hebrews 9:22 say there is no remission without blood?

Hebrews says this because "remission" does not mean "forgiveness." The Greek word is *aphesis*, and it is true that *aphesis* cannot be obtained without blood. The Greek word *aphesis*, often translated "forgiveness," primarily means "release." Yes, it can mean "forgiveness," but if you translate it "forgiveness" in Hebrews 9:22, you make the verse teach something that is not true.

I normally try to avoid explaining my teachings based on Greek words because I am not qualified to do so. *Aphesis*, though, is a critically important Greek word, so I am going to tackle it with the help of several Lexicons, other verses in the New Testament, and the Greek translation of the Old Testament known as the Septuagint.

Aphesis

When I want to see an accurate English definition of a Greek word, I go to https://studybible.info. There I click on "Greek Interlinear," and when I get to the interlinear, I type in the verse I am looking for. The verse shows up with the Greek on top and an English translation below. The Greek words have the Strong's numbers above them, and if you click on that number, you get an immense amount of information about the Greek word.

I did this for Hebrews 9:22 and the word *aphesis*.

- *A Greek Lexicon* by Liddell and Scott Greek English Lexicon, probably the most respected lexicon, gives "a letting go, dismissal" as the first definition.
- The Dodson Greek-English Lexicon has "deliverance, pardon, complete forgiveness, a sending away, a letting go, a release" as the first definition.
- Strong's Concordance gives "freedom; (figuratively) pardon."
- The Tyndale Brief Lexicon of Extended Strong's for Greek gives "dismissal; release" and a reference to Luke 4:18, which we will cover shortly, as a first definition.
- Thayer's Lexicon gives "release from bondage or imprisonment" as the first definition.

As you can see, not a single lexicon lists "forgiveness" as the primary translation of *aphesis* except the Dodson Greek-English

Lexicon, which includes "forgiveness" among six possibilities in its first definition.

Seeing these definitions and having already shown you that God's only requirement for forgiveness is repentance followed by obedience, I feel free to question the idea that there is no "forgiveness" without the shedding of blood.

There is even stronger evidence that Hebrews 9:22 concerns something much larger that forgiveness.

Aphesis in the Septuagint

The Septuagint, the Greek version of the Old Testament translated in the third and second centuries B.C., uses the word *aphesis* to translate the Hebrew words for Jubilee (Lev. 25), the seven-year release from debt and slavery (Deut. 15), and the scapegoat (Lev. 16).

A simple internet search will show that there is some disagreement about just how much Paul and other New Testament writers quoted the Septuagint, but there is no disagreement that it was a lot. Scholars also agree that the Septuagint was the Old Testament of all the churches of Roman Empire, outside Jerusalem, throughout the first and second centuries.

We know that the writer of Hebrews knew about and used the Septuagint. As just one example he quotes Deuteronomy 32:43 from the Septuagint, "Let all the angels of God worship him," in Hebrews 1:6. You will not find this sentence in your Bible because popular English translations are all made from Hebrew manuscripts of the Old Testament. The writer of Hebrews, however, was using the Septuagint.

The point of this is that the writer of Hebrews knew that when he wrote "*aphesis*," his readers would not merely think of forgiveness, which would be represented by the scapegoat from Leviticus 16. His readers would also think of a release from slavery and from all debts, as well as Jubilee, when all land in Israel reverted to the original families who received the land from Joshua when Israel conquered the Promised Land.

Yes, *aphesis* includes forgiveness, but it is so much more! It is restoration to our original land, the elimination of debt, and release from slavery. In the case of a Christian, this represents a return to fellowship with God (all the way back to Eden rather than just back to Joshua's division of the Promised Land), the elimination of guilt (the debt of sin), and release from slavery to sin. Our former slavery to sin, from which grace frees us, is described in Ephesians 2:1-3:

> ... you were dead in transgressions and sins, in which you once walked according to the course of this world, according to the prince of the power of the air, the spirit who now works in the children of disobedience. We also all once lived among them in the lusts of our flesh, doing the desires of the flesh and of the mind, and were by nature children of wrath, even as the rest.

This slavery to sin, rather than only the forgiveness of sin, is what required blood. Jesus' blood is what restored us to fellowship with God, putting us back in God's favor. Paul goes on to describe our deliverance from this slavery by writing:

> But God, being rich in mercy, for his great love with which he loved us, even when we were dead through our trespasses, made us alive together with Christ—by grace you have been saved. (Eph. 2:4-5)

We needed much more than forgiveness, we needed resurrection from the dead! If forgiveness were all that we needed, God could simply have forgiven us. He did not need blood! He did not merely want to forgive us, however; he wanted us to stop sinning. Jesus' blood was required for such a great deliverance, which resurrected us in Christ after we were dead in our sins, and which delivered us from our slavery to sin.

Jesus described his mission to earth, and he used *aphesis* twice in doing so:

> The Spirit of the Lord is on me, because he has anointed me to preach good news to the poor. He has sent me to heal the broken hearted, to proclaim *aphesis* to the captives, recovering of sight to the blind, to send the crushed an *aphesis*, and to proclaim the acceptable year of the Lord. (Luke 4:18-19)

Aphesis is at the very heart of what Jesus came for, and in his own explanation of his mission, *aphesis* is primarily release, not forgiveness. The captives are "released," and the crushed are "delivered." They need more than forgiveness. Forgiveness was already available as a central thought in the Old Testament, but God's Son came to bring deliverance and restoration as well. Thus, Paul writes:

> For the grace of God has appeared, bringing salvation to all men, instructing us to the intent that, denying ungodliness and worldly lusts, we would live soberly, righteously, and godly in this present age; looking for the blessed hope and appearing of the glory of our great God and Savior, Jesus Christ, who gave himself for us, that he might redeem us from all iniquity, and purify for himself a people for his own possession, zealous for good works. (Tit. 2:11-14)

This is what it means when both Ephesians 1:7 and Colossians 1:14 say, "in whom we have our redemption through his blood, the *aphesis* of our trespasses, according to the riches of his grace." Jesus' blood did far more than forgive our sins. It was an entire rescue that required his blood. We were released from slavery, from the *dominion* of our trespasses.

> For sin will not have dominion over you. For you are not under law, but under grace. (Rom. 6:14)

The writer of Hebrews agrees with all this, teaching that the route to *aphesis* required *lutrosis*.

> ... through his own blood, [he] entered in once for all into the Holy Place, having obtained eternal redemption. (Heb. 9:12)

"Redemption" is an accurate translation of *lutrosis*, but only if we consider what "redemption" means. One of the meanings, even in English, of "redemption" is "recovery of something pawned or mortgaged." The American Heritage Dictionary even includes, "deliverance upon payment of ransom; rescue."[13]

If we define "redemption" as "deliverance upon payment of ransom; rescue," it is a perfect translation of *lutrosis*, for which the various lexicons at StudyBible.info all give "liberation,"

---

[13] American Heritage Dictionary of the English Language, 5th ed.; cited by Wordnik, (n.d.), "redemption"

"deliverance," or "a ransoming."[14] Jesus did not enter "into the holy place" to get forgiveness, which God has always given to anyone who would repent, but to deliver and rescue us from the dominion of sin.

This complete deliverance, this "great salvation" (Heb. 2:3), is what Jesus died for, and so Paul writes:

> For to this end Christ died, rose, and lived again, that he might be Lord of both the dead and the living. (Rom. 14:9)

and:

> He died for all, that those who live should no longer live to themselves, but to him who for their sakes died and rose again. (2 Cor. 5:15)

We will delve into this further in the chapter on the atonement. There, we will explore the idea that God is so loving and merciful that he sent his Son to ransom us out of slavery to sin rather than so "holy and just" that he had to kill his own Son because of our sin. In other words, I will argue that God is so holy and just *and merciful* that he sent his only begotten Son to deliver us from the ongoing sin that was the only thing holding back God's forgiveness towards us.

I think, though, that this has been enough of an introduction to prepare you to consider the Bible's description of "God's firm foundation" as a much better alternative to the Calvinist one that we have been bulldozing through these first 20 pages. Let's begin by laying the only foundation that can be laid, Jesus Christ, and find out just what the Scriptures say about *standing on* that foundation.

---

[14] studybible.info, n.d., " G3085 λύτρωσις - Strong's Greek Lexicon Number"

2. Building on the Right Rock

Now when Jesus came into the parts of Caesarea Philippi, he asked his disciples, saying, "Who do men say that I, the Son of Man, am?"

They said, "Some say John the Baptizer, some, Elijah, and others, Jeremiah, or one of the prophets."

He said to them, "But who do you say that I am?"

Simon Peter answered, "You are the Christ, the Son of the living God."

Jesus answered him, "Blessed are you, Simon Bar Jonah, for flesh and blood has not revealed this to you, but my Father who is in heaven. I also tell you that you are Peter, and on this rock I will build my Church, and the gates of Hades will not prevail against it. I will give to you the keys of the Kingdom of Heaven, and whatever you bind on earth will have been bound in heaven; and whatever you release on earth will have been released in heaven." (Matthew 16:13-18)

Roman Catholics love this passage. They claim that the pope is the sole heir of these promises to Peter.[15] The Protestant reaction is to focus on proving that Peter is not the rock. We argue that the rock is really Peter's confession, or we argue that Peter never went to Rome. We argue *against* Roman Catholic teaching, but that is the extent of our dealing with the passage. We focus on what it *does not* mean and, as a result, miss what it *does* mean.

Notice the word "rock" in the passage. When we ignore this passage, we are ignoring something foundational. Jesus said he was going to build his Church on that rock!

If Jesus is building his church on something, then we should be cooperating with him. When we establish churches, we are not building them in our own name. We are building in Jesus' name. We should build our churches on the right rock!

As it turns out, we do not have to argue with the Roman Catholics about which rock to build upon. While they do argue that

---

[15] I refute Rome's claim in Pavao, 2019, *Rome's Audacious Claim*.

Peter is the rock, they agree that Peter's confession is also the rock. Their Catechism says:

> Moved by the grace of the Holy Spirit and drawn by the Father, we believe in Jesus and confess: "You are the Christ, the Son of the living God." On the rock of this faith confessed by St. Peter, Christ built his Church.[16]

Though it is not important to my point in this chapter, we do need to fear the idea that Peter, too, is rightly called "Rock." Peter was the first person to make the confession that Jesus is the Christ, the Son of the living God. That confession is the rock on which Jesus is building his Church, and Peter was the first one to make that confession. When he did so, he became the first of many "living stones" (1 Pet. 2:5) to be laid on the foundation of Jesus Christ. This is enough for Jesus to have named him "Rock."[17]

You do not have to agree with the way I resolve the conflict, but if you are a follower of Jesus, you do have to agree that Matthew 16:13-18 is important. In fact, you must admit that when Jesus talks about a rock and building on it, the passage is *foundational* ... which leads me to this question.

If Peter's confession is the rock on which Jesus builds his Church, why aren't we building our churches on the same confession?

You might argue that Protestant churches do build on the rock because they all believe that Jesus is the Christ, the Son of the living God. In return, I argue that it is one thing to believe this and quite another to build your church on it.

Over my 38 years as a Christian, my range of fellowship has run from several Pentecostal denominations to independent

---

[16] Roman Catholic Church, 2012, *Catechism of the Catholic Church*, par. 424

[17] Some Protestants argue that Peter was not named "Rock," but "Pebble." They argue that the Greek *petra* is a large boulder, but *petros*, which Peter was named, means a small rock, even a pebble. This is inaccurate. Jesus said Peter would be named *Petros* rather than *Petra* because *Petros* is masculine, and *Petra* is feminine. While Bible lexicons give a definition to the word *Petros*, the best lexicon, Liddell and Scott, has no record that the masculine version was ever used in Greek except as a name (Moore, 2007-2021, "Πέτρος, -ου, ὁ").

charismatic churches to Baptist to "non-denominational" churches, which are usually charismatic, and has included interaction with Presbyterians and Methodists. Across the board, all of them have been building their churches on the confession that Jesus died for their sins rather than on the confession that Jesus is the Christ, the Son of the living God.

I suspect your experience has been the same. Have you ever run across "the two questions" in an evangelism training program? They were taught to me in both evangelism training courses I have taken, *Evangelism Explosion* [18] and *Continuing Witness Training* [19]. The two questions are:

1. Do you know for certain you are going to heaven?
2. If you were to die tonight, and God asked you, "Why should I let you into my heaven?" What would you say?

The answer we were taught to look for was anything that had to do with Jesus dying for our sins. "The blood of Jesus" would have been a perfect answer for us. Jesus, we are taught, bought our way into heaven, so if we are going to go out witnessing, you need to tell people that Jesus died for their sins. Everyone knows that.

Everyone except the apostles.

Many years ago, I did a Wednesday evening radio program in Sacramento. One day I decided to compare our modern Gospel with that of the apostles on the air. I did not have Dr. Kennedy's *Evangelism Explosion* on hand, nor much money, so I went to a Christian bookstore and purchased twenty-three different Gospel tracts. I went home and outlined the Gospel message in each one. Since a couple were testimony tracts, no one item was on every tract, but twenty-one of the twenty-three covered the fact that Jesus died for our sins. Since the epistles are written to Christians and the Gospels were too long to outline, I went through the Book of Acts to outline any Gospel presentations that were in it.

I did not expect, nor was I prepared for, what I found.

Before you throw this book away, let me strongly affirm that I believe that Jesus died for our sins. Ephesians 1:7 says, "In [Jesus]

---

[18] Kennedy, 1970
[19] Southern Baptist Convention, 1982

we have redemption through his blood, the forgiveness of our trespasses." Colossians 1:14 repeats that.

Jesus told us to eat a meal in his memory. When he did so, he lifted a cup and said, "This is my blood of the New Covenant, which is poured out for many for the remission of sins" (Matt. 26:28). Not only did Jesus die for our sins, but we are supposed to remember it every time we break the bread and drink the cup of communion. Jesus' death for our sins is all over the New Testament ... except in the preaching of the apostles in the book of Acts.

It is not that it is absent from Acts. Acts 20:28 says, "Take heed, therefore, to yourselves and to all the flock, in which the Holy Spirit has made you overseers, to shepherd the assembly of the Lord and God which he purchased with his own blood." This passage just highlights my point, though. When the apostles spoke or wrote to Christians, they brought up the atonement regularly. It is absent, however, from every sermon the apostles preached to the lost. The one exception is Philip preaching to the Ethiopian eunuch in Acts 8. Because the eunuch was reading Isaiah 53, we have to assume that Philip included the atonement in his Gospel message. We can only assume; it is not said.

The other eleven times that the apostles preached the Gospel to a non-Christian in Acts, the central topic was the resurrection. They mentioned that Jesus died, of course, because no one can rise from the dead without dying. Nonetheless, not one of the Gospel sermons in Acts mentions that the purpose of his death was the remission of sins.

I was every bit as stunned to find this out as you probably are. In no way did I expect the atonement to be omitted when I began outlining Gospel preaching to the lost in the Book of Acts.

Because I have 25 years of experience with evangelical reactions to this simple truth, I want to affirm again that the apostles did teach atonement through Jesus' blood, but *to the churches and not to the lost*! To the lost they emphasized the resurrection that proved Jesus was "the Christ, the Son of the living God" as Peter confessed. Sometimes they used "Lord" (Acts 2:16) or "Judge" (Acts 17:31), but the point was that the resurrection established his authority over all humans.

I acknowledge and teach that the apostles wrote about the atonement throughout their letters to the churches, i.e., to Christians. I am simply pointing out the fact—the easily verifiable fact—that the apostles never told a lost person that Jesus died for his or her sins. Or, if they did, it is not recorded in the Bible.

Surely this difference between the apostles' Gospel preaching and ours is important. The apostles emphasized the resurrection, often to the exclusion of the atonement, while we would never consider preaching the Gospel without including the atonement.

The apostles were building their churches on the same rock that Jesus said he would build his Church on, the confession that Jesus is the Christ, the Son of the living God. John stated that this was the whole point of the stories in his Gospel:

> Jesus did many other signs in the presence of his disciples, which are not written in this book; but these are written, that you may believe that Jesus is the Christ, the Son of God, and that believing you may have life in his name. (Jn. 20:30-31)

That life, says John, is for those who become rocks—living stones (1 Pet. 2:4-6)—the way Peter did, by believing that Jesus is Christ and Son of God. The resurrection proves Jesus is Christ and Lord, which is what the lost need to believe. The atonement could be explained later, after hearers had been saved by believing in their heart that God raised Jesus from the dead and confessing with their mouths that he was Lord (Rom. 10:9-10).

Peter set the example the very first time the Gospel was preached after Jesus died. He announced:

> "Men of Israel, hear these words! Jesus of Nazareth, a man approved by God to you by mighty works and wonders and signs which God did by him among you, even as you yourselves know, him, being delivered up by the determined counsel and foreknowledge of God, you have taken by the hand of lawless men, crucified and killed; ..." (Acts 2:22-23)

Peter told them that they crucified Jesus "by the determined counsel and foreknowledge of God." What a perfect opportunity to explain the atonement to them! Peter, however, neglects the opportunity, jumping straight to the resurrection.

"... whom God raised up, having freed him from the agony of death, because it was not possible that he should be held by it." (v. 24)

After presenting prophecies of the resurrection from Psalms, Peter gives his reason for focusing on the resurrection.

"Let all the house of Israel therefore know certainly that God has made him both Lord and Christ, this Jesus whom you crucified." (v. 36)

In the first Gospel sermon ever preached by the Church, Peter mentions Jesus' death as part of an accusation that the Jews had killed their own Messiah, then spends a dozen verses on the resurrection. This is because the resurrection proves that Jesus is Lord and Christ (Acts 2:36). It was important for Peter to prove that Jesus is Lord and Christ because Jesus was and is building his Church on the confession that Jesus is the Christ, the Son of God!

Peter focused his Gospel preaching on what Jesus called "the rock," but there was another reason Peter emphasized the resurrection.

We all know that Jesus promised the apostles that once the Holy Spirit came upon them, they would be his witnesses (Acts 1:8). What not many of us ask is, witnesses to what? The answer to that question is that Peter and the other apostles were witnesses of the resurrection. Acting as witnesses of the resurrection was possibly their most important role! Their role as witnesses of the resurrection is mentioned in each of the first five chapters of Acts.

1. Of the men therefore who have accompanied us all the time that the Lord Jesus went in and out among us, beginning from the baptism of John, to the day that he was received up from us, of these one must become a witness with us of his resurrection (Acts 1:21-22).
2. This Jesus God raised up, to which we all are witnesses (Acts 2:32).
3. You denied the Holy and Righteous One, and asked for a murderer to be granted to you, and killed the Prince of life, whom God raised from the dead, to which we are witnesses (Acts 3:14-15).

4. With great power, the apostles gave their testimony of the resurrection of the Lord Jesus. Great grace was on them all (Acts 4:33).
5. The God of our fathers raised up Jesus, whom you killed, hanging him on a tree. God exalted him with his right hand to be a Prince and a Savior, to give repentance to Israel, and remission of sins. We are His witnesses of these things; and so also is the Holy Spirit, whom God has given to those who obey him (Acts 5:30-32).

The reason that the apostles were specifically witnesses of the resurrection is because, as Peter said in Acts 2:36, the resurrection proves that Jesus is Lord, Christ, and Son of God. The Apostle Paul agrees, writing "[He] was declared to be the Son of God with power, according to the Spirit of holiness, by the resurrection from the dead" (Rom. 1:4).

There are two more passages in Acts like the five quoted above (10:40-42; 13:30-31), but these are enough. The apostles were witnesses of the resurrection because the resurrection proves that Jesus is the Christ, the Son of God, the rock on which Jesus builds his Church (Matt. 16:16-18).

For example, the apostles testified in Acts 5 to the religious leaders of Jerusalem, who were not willing hearers of the Gospel (vv. 24-28). Peter told the assembled council that God raised Jesus from the dead after "you" killed him on a tree (v. 30). He then used words very similar to his sermon on the day of Pentecost, testifying, "God exalted him with his right hand to be a Prince and a Savior" (v. 31). Peter indicates the purpose of this was "to give repentance to Israel and remission of sins" (v. 31).

Remission of sins is mentioned in this passage, but Peter does not tell the Pharisees that remission of sins is tied to Jesus' death. In fact, he implies that it is tied to the resurrection and his role as Prince and Savior. The apostles' letters do tie the remission of sins to Jesus' death (Eph. 1:7; Col. 1:14), but Peter does not tell the Pharisees that. The same holds true when Peter preaches to Cornelius in Acts 10:

> We are witnesses of everything he did both in the country of the Jews, and in Jerusalem; whom they also killed, hanging him on a tree. God raised him up the third day, and gave him to be

revealed, not to all the people, but to witnesses who were chosen before by God, to us, who ate and drank with him after he rose from the dead. He commanded us to preach to the people and to testify that this is he who is appointed by God as the Judge of the living and the dead. All the prophets testify about him, that through his name everyone who believes in him will receive remission of sins. (vv. 39-43)

Once again, Peter preaches that the Jews crucified Jesus, but he skips the opportunity to explain that his death is for the remission of sins. He goes straight to the resurrection. Then he told Cornelius that God commanded the apostles to testify to the resurrection and preach that he is Judge of the living and dead. He goes from there to the remission of sins, but he ties the release from sins to Jesus' name rather than his death.

The point of all of this is that Jesus is building his Church on the confession that he is the Christ, the Son of God. The atonement is true, important, and is a central part of the apostles' teaching to the churches, but it is not what they preached to the lost.

Notice, too, that the terminology is not what is important, but the proclamation of who Jesus is. Peter did not specifically say "Christ, the Son of God" in his sermon on the day of Pentecost. He said that Jesus is "Christ and Lord." He did not specifically say "Christ, the Son of God" to Cornelius. He said Jesus is "Judge of the living and dead." Paul chose to refer to Jesus as Judge rather than Christ when preaching to Greek philosophers on Mars Hill. In doing so, he follows the apostolic pattern and cites the resurrection as proof (Acts 17:30-31).

More Reasons to Build on the Right Rock

The most important reason to build on the right rock is because that is what Jesus wants us to do and what the apostles did. We should always do what Jesus wants, and we should always follow the apostles' example. There are, though, additional reasons to build on the right rock.

When Paul talked about the resurrection as proof that Jesus is the Son of God, he said that he preached this to bring about "obedience of faith" among the Gentiles (Rom. 1:5). If you preach that Jesus is Christ and Son of God, then it is obvious how to obey that faith. We follow his teachings and obey his commands to the best of our ability.

If, though, a lost person believes that Jesus has died for his sins, how does that person obey that faith? There is nothing to obey. He has acknowledged a fact that calls for no action except belief. Building on the atonement opens the door to the paradoxical idea that one can be a Christian without obeying Christ.

The idea that one can be a Christian without obeying Christ is common in evangelical churches, but it is specifically rejected by Jesus and his apostles. James wrote a half a chapter against it (James 2:14-26), and Paul wrote, "They profess that they know God, but by their deeds they deny him, being abominable, disobedient, and unfit for any good work." (Tit. 1:16). Jesus himself said, "Who do you call me, 'Lord, Lord,' and don't do the things that I say" (Luke 6:46).

This all makes sense if faith is believing that Jesus is the Christ, the Son of the living God. Everyone who believes this about Jesus will at least try to obey him.

In evangelical churches, we try to resolve the problem of believers who do not even try to obey Jesus by saying we are saved if we *really* believe. Or we look at the Greek word for faith and try to define it in a way that includes obedience. We do this because we all know it is absurd to say we believe in Jesus while ignoring what he taught.

The problem is rightly resolved by preaching the right faith. If we preach Jesus as Christ, Lord, and Son of God, then it will be clear that only those who try to obey him actually believe our message.

Paul gives a description of saving faith that is relevant to this topic. Like Peter, he quotes Joel's prophecy that all who call upon the Lord will be saved (Acts 2:21) but, before the quote, he explains what calling on the Lord is:

> If you will confess with your mouth that Jesus is Lord and believe in your heart that God raised him from the dead, you will be saved. For with the heart, one believes unto

righteousness; and with the mouth confession is made unto salvation. (Romans 10:9-10)

Amazingly, this passage has often been used to justify the "sinner's prayer," in which a person tells God he believes Jesus died for his sins and wants Jesus to come into his heart. This passage does not mention Jesus' death, our sins, or Jesus coming into our heart. Instead, it focuses on the resurrection and Jesus as Lord. It also tells us that it is confession that leads to salvation. Since we already know from Matthew 16:16-18 that Jesus is building his church on a confession, this is no surprise. The confession is that Jesus is Lord, and it is based on the belief that Jesus rose from the dead. What a remarkable parallel to everything we have seen so far.

The distinction between the preaching of the apostles and the preaching of modern evangelicals is important. Our modern preaching does not offer a faith that can be obeyed, and it produces a confession different than the confession prescribed by Jesus (Matt. 16:16-18), Peter (Acts 2:36), John (Jn. 20:31), and Paul (Rom. 10:9-10).

The distinction between apostolic preaching and modern preaching produces practical differences as well. Peter's preaching on the day of Pentecost produced three thousand people who "continued steadfastly" in the apostles' teaching, fellowship, breaking of bread, and prayers. Today's preaching produces converts who are indistinguishable from the world on a statistical basis.

> The findings in numerous national polls conducted by highly respected pollsters like The Gallup Organization and The Barna Group are simply shocking. "Gallup and Barna," laments evangelical theologian Michael Horton, "hand us survey after survey demonstrating that evangelical Christians are as likely to embrace lifestyles every bit as hedonistic, materialistic, self-centered, and sexually immoral as the world in general:" Divorce is *more* common among "born-again" Christians than in the general American population. Only 6 percent of evangelicals tithe. White evangelicals are the *most* likely people to object to neighbors of another race. Josh McDowell has pointed out that the sexual promiscuity of evangelical youth is

only a little less outrageous than that of their nonevangelical peers.[20]

The evangelical reply to this charge is that the apostles' churches were not perfect, either. This is true, but Paul could tell even the troubled church in Corinth that they should "purge out the old leaven" by putting wicked ones out of their church (1 Cor. 5:7-13). History testifies that they did an excellent job of purging the leaven. Sometime between A.D. 81 and 96, the church of Rome wrote the following to the church in Corinth:

> For who ever dwelt even for a short time among you, and did not find your faith to be as fruitful of virtue as it was firmly established? Who did not admire the sobriety and moderation of your godliness in Christ? Who did not proclaim the magnificence of your habitual hospitality? ... Moreover, ye were all distinguished by humility, ... yielded obedience rather than extorted it, and were more willing to give than to receive. ... ye were inwardly filled with His doctrine, and His sufferings were before your eyes. Thus a profound and abundant peace was given to you all, and ye had an insatiable desire for doing good, while a full outpouring of the Holy Spirit was upon you all.[21]

On the other hand, my father-in-law, who has been a Southern Baptist pastor and active member for more than 40 years, told me with a tinge of sadness in his voice that he had never seen a church of his denomination carry out the disciplinary instructions in 1 Corinthians 5. If you are an evangelical, and you are surprised by this, then you are in a unique church indeed!

Admittedly, building on the wrong rock is only one reason that evangelical churches have mostly nominal members. We will address another major problem when we talk about the church in chapter four. The wrong foundation, though, is the most critical problem.

---

[20] Sider, 2005, *The Scandal of the Evangelical Conscience*, p. 13; italics in original. My note: tithing is not a New Testament principle, but that does not take away from the import of this quote because most evangelicals think it is.

[21] Clement of Rome, c. 81-96, "First Clement," chs. 1-2

If you, dear reader, continue to found churches on the confession that Jesus died for our sins, you will continue to reap the kind of problems you see in evangelical churches. The wrong root is always going to produce the wrong fruit (cf. Matt. 7:15-20).

With that in mind, it is time to take a deeper look at the foundations of the Christian faith as described in the New Testament.

3. God's Firm Foundation

This chapter is a simple walk through what the Bible describes as "God's Firm Foundation."

Let's begin with a thought experiment. You are introduced to a group of new Christians. These Christians are born again. They have confessed that Jesus is the Christ, the Son of the living God (Matt. 16:16-18). They have repented, been baptized, and they have received the Holy Spirit (Acts 2:38). Their conversion was real, and they are excited to follow Jesus. The person who introduced you to these Christians gives you an opportunity to write two sentences—just two—to start these new believers on their walk of faith, launching them into their new life in Christ.

Do not be intimidated by this. I do not expect you to guess the two sentences inscribed on "God's firm foundation." In fact, I am convinced Paul himself might have chosen different sentences on a different day. Nonetheless, it will be helpful to have two sentences of your own to compare with Paul's.

Stop here and compose two sentences you think are most foundational for a new Christian. Do this before you go on. The next page is blank so that you can compose your sentences without reading ahead.

Do you have your sentences?

Here are the apostle Paul's two sentences:

1. The Lord knows those who are his.
2. Let everyone who names the name of the Lord depart from unrighteousness.

The two sentences are from 2 Timothy 2:19, where Paul tells us they are inscribed on "God's firm foundation."

We are going to examine the purpose of those two sentences throughout this book, though I will be emphasizing only the second one. Comparing your sentences with Paul's will help you decide how much, or perhaps how little, your thinking needs to be adjusted to conform to Paul's.

Second Timothy 2:19 begins with "however." The previous verses mention two men, Hymenaeus and Alexander. Those two men said that the resurrection had already happened, and they overthrew the faith of some (vv. 17-18). 2 Timothy 2:19 is not only answering those two men, however. Hymenaeus and Alexander are two of a class of men whose words are "empty chatter," produce "ungodliness," and "consume like gangrene" (vv. 16-17a). Paul has been addressing this kind of people throughout his letters to Timothy.[22]

2 Timothy 2:19 is an alternative to what Hymenaeus, Alexander, and others like them teach. Throughout the two letters to Timothy, Paul offered very similar alternatives to the teachings of corrupt men.

- "The goal of the command is love out of a pure heart and a good conscience and sincere faith" (1 Tim. 1:5).
- Hold "faith and a good conscience" (1 Tim. 1:19).
- "Flee these things, and follow after righteousness, godliness, faith, love, patience, and gentleness" (1 Tim. 6:11).
- "Flee from youthful lusts, but pursue righteousness, faith, love, and peace with those who call on the Lord out of a pure heart" (2 Tim. 2:22).
- "The Lord's servant must not quarrel, but be gentle to all, able to teach, patient, in gentleness correcting those who oppose him" (2 Tim. 2:24-25).

---

[22] 1 Timothy 1:3-4, 6-7, 19-20; 6:3-6, 20-21; 2 Timothy 2:14, 23-26; 3:1-9

- "But you did follow my teaching, conduct, purpose, faith, patience, love, steadfastness, persecutions, and sufferings" (2 Tim. 3:10).

Look again at Paul's answers to the empty chatter, ungodliness, and gangrene of the teachings of corrupt men. The theme throughout 1 and 2 Timothy is that the Lord's servant should avoid all these theological disputes, which do not lead to godliness, and focus on the things which do.

Thus, 2 Timothy 2:19 fits right into the context of both letters. There exists a class of men like Hymenaeus and Alexander whose empty chatter eats away at godliness like gangrene (vv. 16-18); "however," God's Firm Foundation stands (v. 19), teaching us that The Lord knows those who are his and that everyone who names the name of the Lord must depart from unrighteousness" (v. 19).

This brings us back to the commands to Timothy listed above. They can be summarized as: "Don't be dragged into arguments, but pursue love, faith, godliness, a good conscience, and peace." In other words, "Depart from unrighteousness."

The letters to Timothy and Titus are among the last letters Paul wrote. This is disputed only by those who doubt he wrote them at all.[23] Paul is giving instruction to his two disciples at a time when false teachers were popping up everywhere. His answer throughout is to avoid all the hubbub and stick to training in godliness:

> But refuse profane and old wives' fables. Exercise yourself toward godliness. For bodily exercise has some value, but godliness has value in all things, having the promise of the life which is now, and of that which is to come. This saying is faithful and worthy of all acceptance. For to this end we both labor and suffer reproach, because we have set our trust in the living God, who is the Savior of all men, especially of those who believe. (1 Tim. 4:7-10)

---

[23] "It may be safely predicted that the alternative of placing [the pastoral epistles] at the close of the Apostle's life, or of abandoning the Pauline authorship, will be accepted by both impugners and defenders alike, as common ground." (Bible Study Tools, 2018, "The Date of the Pastoral Epistles").

This is the context of Paul's assertion that God's Firm Foundation is inscribed with "The Lord knows those who are his" and "Let everyone who names the name of the Lord depart from unrighteousness." Corrupt teachers abounded, focusing on all sorts of worthless disputes. These do not lead to godliness. Instead, Paul wanted Timothy and Titus to focus on departing from unrighteousness.

We have not addressed "The Lord knows those who are his." This will come up naturally in the last chapter, as we discuss the practical application of the teachings in this book.

The Foundation of God

We have looked at what is inscribed on God's Firm Foundation. Surely it is even more important to identify the foundation of God itself.

We all know, of course, that "No one can lay any other foundation than that which has been laid, which is Jesus Christ" (1 Cor. 3:11). It is clear, then, that God's Firm Foundation is Jesus Christ. We all agree that to be Christian is to be founded on Jesus Christ.

We may, however, dispute what it means to be standing on the foundation that is Jesus Christ, both as a church and personally. Knowing there is no other foundation than Jesus Christ is not the same as standing on him. To borrow James' wording, even the demons know that Jesus is the only Christian foundation, but they are not standing on that foundation! (Jas. 2:19).

We have Jesus' words to Peter in Matthew 16:16-18. He told us that the Church is going to be built on the foundation of Peter's confession that Jesus is the Christ, the Son of the living God. We can be confident, therefore, that we are initially established on God's Firm Foundation if we confess Jesus as Lord like Peter did and believe in our hearts that God raised him from the dead (Rom. 10:9-10).

Our Lord has one more very clear thing to say about standing on God's Firm Foundation:

> "Everyone therefore who hears these words of mine, and does them, I will liken him to a wise man, who built his house on a

rock. The rain came down, the floods came, and the winds blew, and beat on that house; and it didn't fall, for it was founded on the rock." (Matt. 7:24-25)

If we want our spiritual house to stand on the Rock of Ages, we need to hear his words and do them.

Scripture's words about God's Firm Foundation are consistent ... and perhaps frightening. Jesus is the foundation; we stand on that foundation by doing his words; and it is inscribed with a reminder to depart from unrighteousness.

In other words, if you want to stand on the foundation of Jesus Christ, you need to do what he says.

Long experience tells me that every evangelical, no matter how obedient he or she is to Jesus, will respond to what I have just written by reminding me that we are saved by grace, not works.

This is, of course, true. Paul says it several times (Rom. 3:28; Eph. 2:8-9; Tit. 3:5). What I have written in this chapter is also true.

The simple and unfortunate truth is that the descendants of the Reformation have emphasized Paul's occasional words against works so strongly that they no longer understand Paul's emphasis on doing good works. Even more so, they do not understand his passionate warnings against growing weary in good works.

As we build from the ground up, beginning with the astonishing realization that "depart from unrighteousness" is *foundational* to the Christian faith, Paul's "justified by faith apart from works" will slide comfortably into its proper place in the structure that is the Christian faith.

We have begun build on the right rock, the confession that Jesus is Christ and Son of God. In the next chapter, we will learn the great provision God has made to enable us to stand on the foundation of Jesus Christ the way Jesus said to stand on it, by hearing and obeying his words.

4. Rescuing Good Works

We evangelicals all know that we do not have the power to obey Jesus or live a life of good works until we are born again (Rom. 3 & 7). We know that we are saved by grace through faith, not by works (Rom. 3:28; Eph. 2:8-9). This is drilled into us so much that many evangelicals have developed a distaste even for the mention of "good works."

It is the New Testament which tells us that we cannot save ourselves by good works, but the writers of the New Testament do not share the evangelical distaste for good works. In fact, good works are the purpose of the Scriptures, the goal of grace, the result of the atonement, and the product of walking by the Spirit. At least, that is what Paul thought.

The Purpose of the Scriptures

> Every Scripture is God-breathed and profitable for teaching, for reproof, for correction, and for instruction in righteousness, that the man of God may be complete, thoroughly equipped for every good work. (2 Timothy 3:16-17)

Notice that Paul gives several *uses* for the Scriptures. They are profitable for "teaching, for reproof, for correction, and for instruction in righteousness." In other words, you can *use* the Scriptures profitably to teach believers, to reprove them when they have departed from the way, to correct them when they are confused, and to instruct them in the ways of righteousness. But all these uses of Scripture are to achieve a goal: "... that the man of God may be complete, thoroughly equipped for every good work."

That is worth thinking about. The purpose of the Bible is to equip followers of Christ to do good works. It is not the only purpose. The Scriptures surely have more than one purpose. Jesus, for example, said another purpose of the Scriptures is to testify about him (Jn. 5:39). In 2 Timothy 3:16-17, though, the Apostle Paul focuses on the purpose of producing Christians that are thoroughly prepared to do good works.

This sounds strange to our evangelical ears, I know. Surely the atoning death of Christ is far more important than our good works.

And, of course, it is. Jesus' death and resurrection are the focus not only of the Scriptures but of all human history and experience. At the cross, Jesus ended one age, and with his resurrection he inaugurated the age of the children of God. When we are resurrected, and our adoption is fulfilled, the whole creation will be released from its groaning and longing, and not just everyone, but everything, will rejoice at the revelation of the sons of God (Rom. 8:19-23).[24]

The atoning death of Christ is more important than our good works, but it was every bit as much to produce good works in us as the Scriptures are.

The Purpose of the Atonement and Grace

> For the grace of God has appeared, bringing salvation to all men, instructing us to the intent that, denying ungodliness and worldly lusts, we would live soberly, righteously, and godly in this present world; looking for the blessed hope and appearing of the glory of our great God and Savior, Jesus Christ; who gave himself for us, that he might redeem us from all iniquity, and purify for himself a people for his own possession, zealous for good works. (Tit. 2:11-14)

Jesus died to redeem us from iniquity so that he might own a people who are zealous for good works. Just as the purpose of the Scriptures is to equip people of God for good works, so at least one purpose of Jesus' death was to produce a people for himself who would be zealous for good works.

In addition, the grace of God, which Jesus died to bring us into (Jn. 1:16-17; Rom. 5:2; Eph. 2:4-5), is a central tool for producing such a people. The grace that brings salvation teaches us to deny ungodliness and worldly lusts and to live soberly, righteously, and godly in this present age (Tit. 2:11-12). Grace not only teaches us to live this way, but it enables us to do so by eliminating sin's power over us (Rom. 6:14).

---

[24] This paragraph is not theologically precise. "The age of the Sons of God" might better be applied to the next age, after the resurrection. I am just trying to express the magnitude of what Jesus did on the cross, and there are no sufficient words.

So we see that at least one purpose of Jesus' death was to purchase a people who would not only do good works, but be zealous for them. We have seen that one purpose of the Scriptures is to equip us to do good works and grace teaches us and empowers us to do good works. Three of the most important gifts of God—Scripture, the atonement, and grace—all have the purpose of producing good works in us!

It does not stop there. Ephesians 2:8-10 tells us that the new birth is for the purpose of good works.

The Purpose of the New Birth

> For by grace you have been saved through faith, and that not of yourselves; it is the gift of God, not of works, that no one would boast. For we are his workmanship, created in Christ Jesus for good works, which God prepared before that we would walk in them. (Eph. 2:8-10)

In evangelical Christianity we focus on Ephesians 2:8-9. It matters to us immensely that we were saved apart from works. And so it should. Trying to work our way into a new birth, a re-creation, is impossible. No one can "create us in Christ Jesus" except God. Nonetheless, after we have been saved, re-created in Christ Jesus apart from works, our purpose becomes doing the good works that God has prepared for us to do.

We see then that ...

- ... we are [re-]created in Christ Jesus to do good works (Eph. 2:10).
- ... grace comes to teach us to live sensible, godly, and righteous lives (Tit. 2:11-12).
- ... Jesus died to purge us of lawlessness, to purchase us, and to make us zealous for good works (Tit. 2:13-14).
- ... the Scriptures are given to us so that we may be thoroughly equipped for good works (2 Tim. 3:16-17).

I think we can already say that it is no surprise that "let everyone who names the name of the Lord depart from unrighteousness" is engraved on God's firm foundation (2 Tim. 2:19).

Perhaps, then, we should increase our focus on good works. Surely, a people who are being taught by grace to do good works; who are re-created in Christ Jesus to do works God has prepared for them; who are taught by the grace of God to do good works; whom Jesus has purged of lawlessness and made zealous for good works; and who use the Scriptures to equip one another for good works ... surely such a people will love to talk about good works and to teach, reprove, correct, and instruct one another toward good works!

In fact, much talk about good works is exactly what the Apostle Paul prescribed to Titus. Immediately after telling him that Jesus died to obtain a people zealous for good works, he wrote: "Say these things. Exhort and reprove with all authority. Let no man despise you" (Tit. 2:15). A few verses later, he added, "Concerning these things I desire that you affirm confidently, so that those who have believed God may be careful to maintain good works" (Tit. 3:8).

In these days, when trying to do good works is sometimes seen as a hindrance to salvation or to walking with God, it matters that Paul said, "Let no man despise you," when we say these things. The people of God are supposed to be careful to maintain good works, not complain when good works are mentioned! (Tit. 3:8).

Despite all this emphasis on good works we have already seen in the Scripture, we are not done yet! There is more!

The Purpose of Walking by and Sowing to the Spirit

It is a clear and irrefutable teaching of Scripture that good works are the fruit, the product of, "remaining" in Christ (Jn. 15:1-11). The only way to do good works is to "walk after" (Rom. 8:4), "walk by" (Gal. 5:16), and "sow to" (Gal. 6:8) the Spirit. Apart from Jesus, we "can do nothing" (Jn. 15:5).

Through Christ, however, we can do all things (Php. 4:13), and this will not just automatically happen without your effort. Thus, Paul commands Titus to "affirm confidently" (Tit. 3:8) and to "exhort and reprove with all authority" (Tit. 2:15) that we must "be careful to maintain good works." Being careful to maintain something is not waiting around expecting it to happen; no, carefully maintaining good works means actively applying ourselves to doing good. Yes, this includes knowing that the life of Jesus produces these good works in us (cf. Php. 2:13), but it does not exclude working out our salvation with fear and trembling (Php. 2:12) nor "being careful" to maintain good works (Tit. 3:8).

A good picture of the balance of walking by the Spirit and doing good works is in Galatians 6:8-9. In verse 8, we are told that those who "sow to the Spirit" will "reap eternal life." In verse 9, however, he tells us that we must not "be weary of doing good" or "give up" if we hope to reap. If there were none of our effort involved, it would be impossible to grow weary or give up.

Paul described the effort he put into maintaining good works. He wrote:

> Don't you know that those who run in a race all run, but one receives the prize? Run like that, that you may win. Every man who strives in the games exercises self-control in all things. Now they do it to receive a corruptible crown, but we an incorruptible. I therefore run like that, not aimlessly. I fight like that, not beating the air, but I beat my body and bring it into submission, lest by any means, after I have preached to others, I myself should be rejected. (1 Cor. 9:24-27)

If anyone walked by the Spirit, it was the apostle Paul, but he nonetheless trained like an Olympian, subduing his body. He told us to do the same, writing, "If you live after the flesh, you must die; but if by the Spirit you put to death the deeds of the body, you will live" (Rom. 8:13).

We have discussed how the Scriptures, grace, the Holy Spirit, the atonement, and the new birth all point toward and equip us for good works. In this way, God gives us "all things that pertain to life and godliness" (1 Pet. 1:3). Nonetheless, the great and precious gifts we have already discussed are still not all he gives to us! He also equips us for every good work through humans!

The Purpose of Assembling the Church

All evangelicals know that the Bible says, "... not forsaking the assembling of ourselves together" (Heb. 10:25, NKJV). Very few know what we are supposed to do instead of forsaking the assembling of ourselves together. We assume that if we assemble, then we have done what the Bible says. This is not true. Hebrews 10:25 is just one part of a longer sentence.

> And let us consider one another in order to stir up love and good works, not forsaking the assembling of ourselves together, as is the manner of some, but exhorting one another, and so much the more as you see the Day approaching. (Heb. 10:24-25)

Yes, here again the purpose of assembling ourselves as a church is to "stir up love and good works." This is done by "exhorting one another."

We are mistaken when we think that three songs, an offering, and a sermon fulfills Hebrews 10:24-25. It is a wonderful thing for the church to gather to sing. Offerings are wonderful if they are used for good things. It is a wonderful thing for shepherds and teachers to teach the church. None of these things, however, are mentioned in Hebrews 10:24-25. The writer pictures the saints coming together to stir one another up so that we all love and do good. This is not done by a professional speaking to a congregation, but by all of us "exhorting one another." The assembly that the writer of Hebrews has in view is one in which the saints come together to talk and exercise their gifts. He is envisioning 1 Corinthians 14, where "each one of you has a psalm, has a teaching, has a revelation, has another language, or has an interpretation. Let all things be done to build each other up" (v. 26).

Whether you think the gift of speaking in another language has passed away or not, we are commanded by Scripture to assemble for the purpose of exhorting one another and stirring up good works. Even outside of the assembly, the writer of Hebrews tells us to "exhort one another day by day, so long as it is called 'today', lest any one of you be hardened by the deceitfulness of sin" (3:13).

Do not be deceived, as long as we are in the body, we have to work out our salvation in fear and trembling (1 Jn. 3:7; Php. 2:12), and we need to help each other with this task. We must be speaking truth in love to one another (Eph. 4:15), and this must be done by "each individual part" (Eph. 4:16).

With things the way they are, one unhappy side effect of the New Testament emphasis on obedience and good works can be discouragement. Despite all the emphasis I have put on the tremendous gifts God has given us for good works, to live a life of obedience to God seems overwhelming to those of us who have been taught that obedience is optional.

The New Testament makes provision for our failures and faults. Though the gifts of God are given to change us from doers of evil to doers of good, that work is a process which will never end in sinless perfection, but rather in joyous fellowship with our heavenly Father that transforms us from one glory to the next (2 Cor. 3:18). If we continue to the end, God will continue to the end as well, going ever deeper in his work in us.

5. The Mercy of God

The Reformation version of works, sinless perfection, and the final judgment has prevailed for so long that I cannot discuss how God has empowered us for good works without pausing to remind you of the mercy of the God who will judge us on the last day.

> "The Lord! The Lord, a merciful and gracious God, slow to anger, and abundant in loving kindness and truth, keeping loving kindness for thousands, forgiving iniquity and disobedience and sin; and who will by no means clear the guilty, visiting the iniquity of the fathers on the children, and on the children's children, on the third and on the fourth generation." (Ex. 34:6-7)

God's announcement of himself to Moses makes it clear that there is a difference between committing iniquity, disobedience, and sin and being "guilty." Let me repeat that. There is a difference between a guilty person and someone who has committed iniquity, disobedience, or sin. God will forgive the latter, but he will not clear the former.

This is expressed similarly in Galatians 6:7. "Do not be deceived, God is not mocked." There comes a point where someone is not weak, he or she is mocking God in their disobedience. There comes a point where a person did not merely stumble or falter, they are guilty. They are not even trying. They are making a mockery of God's mercy. Persistent and unrepentant in their sin, they will inherit corruption (Gal. 6:8). There will be condemnation and wrath at the final judgment (Rom. 2:5-9; Eph. 5:3-7), but the condemnation and wrath of God is never directed at the weak, but only the rebellious. As he says of himself, God is in the habit of forgiving iniquity, disobedience, and sin (Ex. 34:6-7).

No one is perfectly sinless. The best passage to prove this is 1 John 1:7 through 2:2:

> But if we walk in the light, as he is in the light, we have fellowship with one another, and the blood of Jesus Christ, his Son, cleanses us from all sin. If we say that we have no sin, we deceive ourselves, and the truth is not in us. If we confess our sins, he is faithful and righteous to forgive us the sins, and to

cleanse us from all unrighteousness. If we say that we haven't sinned, we make him a liar, and his word is not in us. My little children, I write these things to you so that you may not sin. If anyone sins, we have a Counselor with the Father, Jesus Christ, the righteous. And he is the atoning sacrifice for our sins, and not for ours only, but also for the whole world.

This is the same apostle who wrote, "Whoever is born of God [is not committing] sin" (1 Jn. 3:9). The Greek verb tense implies that the one born of God has a pattern of not sinning. As a result, the New American Standard Bible translates the verse as saying he "does not practice sin." John said there is an obvious difference between a righteous son of God and a wicked son of the devil (1 Jn. 3:10), but the long passage I just quoted makes it clear he is not talking about sinless perfection. Instead, he is talking about a Spirit-filled person who recognizes sin, repents when he or she has sinned, and presses forward, becoming more and more holy by relying on the grace of God that teaches us to "deny ungodliness and worldly lusts" (Tit. 2:11-12). We should be growing in virtue, knowledge, self-control, perseverance, godliness, brotherly kindness, and love (2 Pet. 1:5-8), but "if anyone sins," we have a Helper with the Father, not a wrathful Judge (1 Jn. 2:2).

Mercy is one of the most emphasized of God's attributes under the Old Covenant. We find the words "his mercy endures forever" 41 times in the Old Testament of the King James Version, including 26 times in Psalm 136. When the Lord fought a battle for King Jehoshaphat against three armies, Jehoshaphat put singers in front of his soldiers. They sang "his mercy endures forever" all the way to their non-battle (2 Chr. 7:6, KJV).[25]

God's everlasting mercy can perhaps be seen best in Jeremiah's lamentation after Judah had disobeyed God so extensively and for so long that God sent them into captivity in Babylon. Even as this judgment was falling on Israel, Jeremiah proclaimed:

---

[25] Many, if not most, modern versions translate this "his lovingkindness endures forever." The Hebrew word can mean "mercy," "lovingkindness," "kindness," and other similar English words. It is directly tied to the forgiveness of sins in Exodus 34:7 and Numbers 14:18-19.

> It is because of the Lord's loving kindnesses that we are not consumed, because his compassion doesn't fail. They are new every morning. Great is your faithfulness. (Lam. 7:22-23)

We are not to panic when we sin. The writer of Hebrews tells us to come with "boldness" to God's throne, where we will find "mercy" and "grace to help in time of need" (Heb. 4:16). The sinlessly perfect do not need mercy. Christians, all of whom stumble in many things (James 3:2), do need mercy. If we come boldly to "the throne of grace," we will obtain not only mercy, but also "grace to help in time of need" (Heb. 4:16).

John similarly promised that when we confess our sins, we get both deliverance *and* cleansing (1 Jn. 1:9). In that verse, the Greek word for "forgive" is *aphiemi*, the verb form of *aphesis*, which we discussed in chapter one and primarily means release. If we confess our sins, he both releases us from captivity to them and purifies us. He gives us both mercy and grace: mercy to cleanse and grace to release us from sin's dominion (Heb. 4:16; Rom. 6:14).

We should only panic when we find ourselves giving up the fight. We must not "grow weary in doing good" (Gal. 6:9). We do not want to be among those who "shrink back to destruction," but among those "who have faith to saving of the soul" (Heb. 10:39).

Paul worked at subduing his body throughout his life (1 Cor. 9:27), and at the end of it, he would tell Timothy, "I have fought the good fight" (2 Tim. 4:7). Peter says that our bodily desires "war against the soul" (1 Pet. 2:11). This is the good fight that Paul fought.

Like Paul, we are trying to win that war. As we have seen, there is a reward of eternal life for those who persevere in doing good (Rom. 2:7) and for those who do not faint (Gal. 6:8-9). The Bible would not need to make such promises if there were not battles and pressures that can cause us to faint. We must not do so. God has given us many gifts, many promises, and many weapons to get us over the hurdles in our life. Paul told his churches that it is "through many afflictions we must enter God's Kingdom" (Acts 14:22).

One of the greatest of those promises and weapons is God's mercy. Jesus told Peter that he must forgive a brother who repents up to 490 times! (Matt. 18:22). Of course, we know Jesus was not giving him an exact number but telling him to forgive each and every time a brother or sister repented to him. Our Father in heaven will not be less merciful than he asks us to be. Just as we cannot be more holy than God, neither can we be more merciful.

Again, we must consider grace when we consider mercy. Grace includes the power that frees us from sin's dominion (Rom. 6:14). Grace teaches us to deny ungodliness and worldly lusts (Tit. 2:11-12). We need both.

God makes an additional provision for us: each other. We are not only to make confession to God, but to our brothers and sisters. It is not that we need a priest to forgive our sin. Instead, we confess our transgressions to one another so our brothers and sisters know how to pray for us. According to James those prayers are "powerfully effective" to heal us (Jas. 5:16).

Addictions

Some sins are rightly called addictions. Both sexual sins and substance abuse fall into this category. Addictions are sometimes healed miraculously by God, but sometimes it is necessary to depend on humans to control us in areas where we do not have self-control. We are in a war against sin, and we must win it. Since pride is such a great sin in and of itself, a sin which will pit God himself against you, humbling yourself to confess an embarrassing or dangerous addiction is a double weapon against your flesh, striking against both your pride and your addiction.

Our war against sin is a lifelong affair. It is not that we should struggle with the same sins decade after decade, and if you take advantage of the promises of God and the help of your brothers and sisters in Christ, you will not do so. Our growth is progressive, and God will be rooting out sin throughout our lifetime. He will begin with the major sins, the ones that hurt others worst, and progress to more minor ones as you progress.

Peter describes this, writing:

> Yes, and for this very cause adding on your part all diligence, in your faith supply moral excellence; and in moral excellence, knowledge; and in knowledge, self-control; and in self-control perseverance; and in perseverance godliness; and in godliness brotherly affection; and in brotherly affection, love. For if these things are yours and abound, they make you to not be idle or unfruitful in the knowledge of our Lord Jesus Christ. (2 Pet. 1:5-8)

In these verses, Peter describes our effort. Other passages remind us of God's efforts. Most of us are familiar with Philippians 2:12-13, where Paul tells us to work out our salvation with fear and trembling but adds that it is God who works in us to desire and to do his good will.

Many of us know Philippians 1:6 and the promise that the one who began a good work in us will continue it until Jesus comes back. Most of Paul's letters include a promise like this. Paul promised the Corinthians that God would confirm them until the end, "blameless in the day of our Lord Jesus Christ" (1 Cor. 1:8). He told the Romans not to judge one another because God is our Master. We are not the judges or rulers of one another. He then adds, "Yes, he will be made to stand, for God is able to make him stand" (Rom. 14:4).

I like to tell my brothers and sisters, the desiring and the effort is your job, the succeeding is God's. Or, more succinctly, if we give God diligence, he will reward that diligence (Heb. 11:6). We are never to lack in diligence, and we must be fervent in spirit (Rom. 12:11), but if we sin despite our best plans and hope and effort, then we may "return to the Lord, and he will have mercy ... to our God, for he will freely pardon" (Isa. 55:7).

God is building and growing us, not perfecting us instantly. God is merciful as we progress, and we must show mercy to one another as we each press forward in faith. It is only the disorderly we are to warn. The faint-hearted and weak, we are to encourage and support (1 Thess. 5:14). God does the same.

Whom Will God Not Charge with Sin?

There is a remarkable comment in Romans 4:8:

> Even as David also pronounces blessing on the man to whom God counts righteousness apart from works, "Blessed are they whose iniquities are forgiven, whose sins are covered. Blessed is the man whom the Lord will by no means charge with sin."

This passage is quoted from Psalm 32:1-2, so it does not just apply to Christians. It also applied under the Old Testament. When King David said a man is blessed if the Lord will not charge him with sin, he was certainly including himself. How would he know about that blessing if he were not experiencing it?

Despite experiencing that blessing, when he crossed a line—when the sin was major enough or when David did not repent—the Lord most certainly charged him with sin. When David sinned with Bathsheba, God did not allow the baby to live, despite David spending a week praying on his face in repentance (2 Sam. 12:1-23). When he took a census of Israel against God's will and the advice of the leaders of his army, God killed 70,000 Israelites (2 Sam. 24). I cannot help but notice that others were punished for David's sin. If you are like me, let me point out that in the first case, David was punished with a reign filled with warfare (2 Sam. 12:10), and in the second case, God intended in advance to punish Israel for their own disobedience (2 Sam. 24:1).

Early in Christian history, in the second century, a Christian reported discussing this issue with a Jew. Apparently, Jews of the second century believed, because of Psalm 32, that if they were circumcised and kept the Sabbath and food laws, God would not charge them with sin.

> So that if they repent, all who wish for it can obtain mercy from God: and the Scripture foretells that they shall be blessed, saying, "Blessed is the man to whom the Lord imputeth not sin;" that is, having repented of his sins, that he may receive remission of them from God; and not as you [Jews] deceive yourselves, and some others who resemble you in this, who say, that even though they be sinners, but know God, the Lord will not impute sin to them. We have as proof of this the one fall of David, which happened through his boasting, which was forgiven then when he so mourned and wept, as it is written. But if even to such a man no remission was granted before repentance, and only when this great king, and anointed one,

and prophet, mourned and conducted himself so, how can the impure and utterly abandoned, if they weep not, and mourn not, and repent not, entertain the hope that the Lord will not impute to them sin?[26]

At least one Christian, around A.D. 160, believe that the person against whom the Lord will not charge sin—or, as the KJV renders it, "will not impute sin"—is the one who repents and mourns and weeps when they sin. I want to argue for a different qualification.

Walking in the Light

The apostle John tells us that if we walk in the light, we will have fellowship with each other and "the blood of Jesus Christ, his Son, cleanses us from all sin" (1 Jn. 1:7). This is the equivalent of telling us that *if we walk in the light*, God will not charge sin to us. Instead, he will cleanse us by the blood of Jesus.

John loved to use the present tense. In Greek, tenses indicate the type of action even more than they indicate time.[27] The present tense indicates ongoing, repeated, or continuous action. Thus, John is saying that if we walk in the light, the blood of Jesus will be cleansing us on an ongoing, repeated, or continuous basis. Surely this is the same as not having our sins charged to us.

Evangelicals who hear me teach on the judgment often ask me, "If we are going to be judged by our works, where's the line? How good is good enough?"

Typically, I will tell them, "There is a reason that God tells us to fear the judgment. You don't know the line. Please him!"

One of my sons likes to tell me, "They are asking the wrong question, and they have their eyes on the wrong thing. They should be asking how they can best please him, and they won't have to worry about the line. We don't want to be near it anyway!"

I may, though, begin telling those who ask that question that they must walk in the light. It is not how much you sin, but whether or not you expose your sin to the light of God. That light

---

[26] Justin Martyr, c. 155-165, *Dialogue with Trypho*, ch. 141
[27] Keating, n.d., "Greek Verb Tenses (Intermediate Discussion)"

is powerful, cleansing, transforming. There are Scriptures that describe this. Ephesians 5 is a good place to start.

> For you were once darkness, but are now light in the Lord. Walk as children of light, for the fruit of the Light[28] is in all goodness and righteousness and truth, proving what is well pleasing to the Lord. Have no fellowship with the unfruitful deeds of darkness, but rather even reprove them. For it is a shame even to speak of the things which are done by them in secret. But all things, when they are reproved, are revealed by the light, for everything that reveals is light. (Eph. 5:8-12).

Two things are said of light here. It reveals, and it produces fruit. We are not surprised that the fruit of the light is "goodness, righteousness, and truth" because we have seen already that walking in the light results in fellowship and purification of sin (1 Jn. 1:7). Let's look at another passage to help us with the idea of revealing:

> "This is the judgment, that the light has come into the world, and men loved the darkness rather than the light; for their works were evil. For everyone who does evil hates the light, and doesn't come to the light, lest his works would be exposed. But he who does the truth comes to the light, that his works may be revealed, that they have been done in God." (John 3:19-21)

This is Jesus, and he also tells us that light exposes. Those who flee to the darkness will be condemned, but the one who "does the truth" wants his works to be revealed by the light.

It is easy to assume here that the one who comes to the light to reveal his deeds has done good deeds, but the passage does not say this. Again, John loves using the Greek present tense to convey habit or a general rule. It is those who have a habit of being truthful who come to the light. Their deeds "have been done in God." The point being made is that those who come to the light are those who habitually, as their normal practice, expose their deeds to God. This is walking in the light, and it produces luscious fruit:

---

[28] The World English Bible has Spirit here, but most modern translations have "light." I used "light" because it makes more sense in context.

goodness, righteousness, truth, fellowship, and a constant purification by the blood of Jesus.

Who are the people to whom God will not charge sin? The ones who walk in the light, who constantly expose their deeds to God, leading to purification and transformation.

We can do nothing without Jesus (Jn. 15:5), but with him, we can expose our deeds to God's light, be forgiven and transformed, and become those who are known for good deeds.

With all that said, unpleasant experience requires me to add the following.

Excursus on Addiction and Sexual Predation

It is important, here, to point out that I am talking about sins that do not harm others in any criminal way. Child molesters need to get professional help, and children need to be protected from them. This is not a rare enough problem, even among Christians. I know too many families that have been through this. God may grant the victims the ability to *forgive* such awful tragedies, but they must never trust the predator again. Children should never be exposed to the perpetrator again except with good cause and constant supervision. Given the opportunity, especially in the same environment, the crime will almost always be repeated. As much as possible, there must be no further occurrences or new victims.

Murder, rape, armed robbery, and other violent crimes fall into the same category. The authorities should deal with such matters, and converts should be instructed to turn themselves over to the police or a lawyer. A jail or a rehab facility will not prevent us from serving them with the Gospel, friendship, and teaching.

My point here is that there are some sins that are such a danger to society that it is inappropriate to deal slowly with the sin through love, friendship, guidance, and exhortation. Some sins require love, guidance, exhortation, ***and*** confinement, whether in a prison or a rehab program. Please let those who need confinement be confined.

Now that we have established the importance of good works and living in God's mercy by walking in the light, let's discuss just what the term "good works" means!

6. Which Good Works?

Personally, I think the definition of good works is simple. Good works are things we do that are good. Before we unpack that, however, I need to talk about what good works are *not*.

Evangelism Is Not the Only Good Work

One of my favorite Christian singers is Carman. His music is peppy and focused on bold confidence in the Lord. He released his first album the year I became a Christian, and I have been listening to his music for 38 years since. In one of his songs, "Overcomin' Child of God," he sings:

> God wants us to share the Lord
> Isn't that our Christian task?[29]

This is a rhetorical question. Carman is confident that his listeners can only answer yes. We all know that sharing the Lord is one of the most important reasons we are on the earth. There are some, though, who apparently believe witnessing for the Lord is the *only* reason we are on earth.

As a result, when I talk to people about good works, their minds jump to Jehovah's Witnesses going door-to-door. They imagine going to church more, giving to missions more, joining their church's visitation team, and disrupting co-workers to "share the Lord" every day.

Except for disrupting co-workers (1 Thess. 4:11), there is nothing wrong with those things. Nonetheless, sharing the Lord is not "our Christian task"; it is *one of* our Christian tasks.

You can scour the letters to the churches in the New Testament, and the only commands to witness to our neighbors must be teased out of vague inferences. For example, a favorite witnessing verse when I was being discipled by the Navigators[30] was Philemon 1:6: "… that the communication of thy faith may

---

[29] Carman. (2005). "Live & Reloaded!" Album. Alliant Music Group.

[30] The Navigators is an evangelism and discipleship ministry that focuses on young people, such as college students and military personnel. See https://www.navigators.org/about/ for more information.

become effectual by the acknowledging of every good thing which is in you in Christ Jesus" (KJV). We were told that this meant we should be communicating our faith to others by going out of our way to witness to people.

I do not object to going out of our way to witness to people. I have fond memories of passing out tracts on Miracle Strip in the panhandle of Florida and of drawing illustrations of the atonement on napkins at the Ramstein Air Force Base bowling alley. Nonetheless, Philemon 1:6 is not primarily about evangelism.

Modern versions, like the New American Standard Bible, accurately translate Philemon 1:6 as "... that the *fellowship* of your faith may become effective through the knowledge of every good thing that is in you ..." (italics mine). In verse 5, Paul had just commended Philemon for his faith toward Jesus and his love for all the saints (Phm. 1:5). The fellowship of his faith, i.e., his love for all the saints, was made effective because others saw good things in him. He was not "presenting the Gospel"; he was fellowshipping with the saints. Therefore, in verse 7, Paul says, "the hearts of the saints have been refreshed by you, brother" (NASB).

Philemon 1:6 is not about going door to door with the Gospel; it is akin to what Paul, Silas, and Timothy wrote to the Thessalonians. The Thessalonian Christians became such excellent imitators of the apostles and of the Lord that their example spread all the way to Macedonia and Achaia.[31] As a result, the apostles did not have to say anything because the churches in Macedonia and Achaia already knew the Thessalonians had turned from idols to God (1 Thess. 1:6-9).

They were an excellent example of what Jesus promised to those who would do good works. Their good works were a brilliant light that made the church in Thessalonica shine like a city set on a hill that could not be hidden. Their good works brought glory to their Father in heaven (Matt. 5:14-16).

Interestingly, when some of the Thessalonians decided they needed to evangelize full-time, Paul rebuked them. He called them

---

[31] i.e., from Thessalonica in somewhat central Greece north to Philippi and south to Corinth

busybodies and ordered that they should not be allowed to eat until they went back to work (2 Thess. 3:6-11). Such people were told to work "with quietness" (2 Thess. 3:12). They should have known this from the first letter because the apostles had already told them to love one another and to make it their "ambition" to "lead a quiet life, do your own business, and work with your own hands." It was this behavior that the apostles said qualified as "walking properly towards those who are outside" (1 Thess. 4:9, 11-12).

I know I am kicking over one of the most sacred of evangelical cows: devoting our lives to witnessing. Some Christians are called to do this. God provides evangelists for the churches (Eph. 4:11). He also provides apostles who plant churches, though we call them "missionaries" and "church-planters" today. Apostles must be both evangelists and shepherds because of the work they do. Thus, Timothy, who was helping Paul plant churches, was told to "do the work of an evangelist" so that he could "fulfill [his] ministry" (2 Tim. 4:5). Not everyone has evangelism as their ministry or as part of their ministry.

I have found very few evangelicals open to what I have just written. My argument is that we will reach the world better by obeying Jesus and the apostles than by forming our own plans. Instead of trying to fit all Christians into Paul and Timothy's mold, we should listen to Paul who said, "How can they preach except they be sent?" (Rom. 10:15).

Jesus sent the apostles (Matt. 28:18-20). Yes, Jesus wants the Gospel of the Kingdom to reach the end of the world and for everyone to hear it (Matt. 24:14). He wants us to pray for workers sent into the harvest (Matt. 9:38). He wants new Christians to grow into mature Christians so that he can send those mature, discipled Christians out into the harvest (Rom. 10:15). Further, he wants every Christian to be prepared to answer those who ask us why we hope in Christ (1 Pet. 3:15).

As Christians, of course we want to reach the world with the Gospel. I have been on several mission trips; I support, pray for, and encourage several missionaries. I presented the teaching that grew into this book at a missions conference, asking God to equip the missionaries that were there and their support teams. May God send more and more laborers into his harvest!

I also pray that those who are not sent will not go out into the world because of a command given to eleven apostles! There is a reason Paul said, "How shall they preach unless they be sent?" (Rom. 10:15). Just today a missionary friend wrote on Facebook:

> A friend of mine told me years ago that most missionaries fail. They give up in discouragement. The joys are awesome and the failures are smothering. ... Difficult and challenging times are in store for all that step out to do battle. I know we all love the wonderful testimonies. I love them myself. ... we get such sanitized stories about success sometimes. We get grim reality in failure, I mourn for those that have gone home feeling they failed. I am sad at their disappointment. It is heartbreaking. And again, most fail. As my brother shared, it is the best kept secret in missions.[32]

The cause of this problem is twofold. One, we are sending missionaries that are not equipped for what they will face. Two, many missionaries have been manipulated into feeling called. Because evangelism is, for many evangelicals, the one good work, becoming holy is associated with becoming a missionary.

Consider another story told to me by Richard Jacobson, author of *The Unchurching Comic Book*.[33] He had taken a job as a youth pastor, and he set out to give the youth what he felt they needed, a profound and real experience with God. To do so, he spent months building up their faith and promising that on a specific day they would *really* experience God. Along the way, other youth heard about this promise, and his youth group grew.

When the day came, Richard was terrified. He was worried that God would not show up. He knew he should have faith, of course, but I am sure we all know how hard that can be sometimes. He brought them to a park and told them to go in the woods and pray. He told them that if they saw another youth, to walk the other way. Sit or walk but stay alone and pray. Do not come back until God has spoken to you.

---

[32] Glenn Roseberry; July 6, 2020
[33] Jacobson, 2017, *The Unchurching Comic Book*, available free at http://www.unchurching.com/comic

For several hours, he waited anxiously, imagining newspaper headlines saying, "Youth Pastor Destroys the Faith of Children." Finally, a young man emerged from the woods. Richard asked him what God had told him. He said, "God called me to be a missionary."

Richard told him, "Wonderful! Why don't you go back and see if he says anything else?"

One young person after another came out of the woods, saying they had been called to be a pastor, missionary, nurse, or similar ministry. He sent them all back. This, of course, only accentuated his fears.

Finally, in the early evening, a young man came running out of the woods. He ran right up to Richard and announced, "God spoke to me!"

Richard smiled and asked what he said. The boy got closer and raised his voice, "No, you don't understand, he really spoke to me!!"

This was what Richard was looking for; not a forced or imagined commitment, but a real experience with God.

One by one, more came running out of the woods, the same wide-eyed expression on their faces. As Richard told my wife and me about that day, his voice got soft, and he asked, "Do you know what God said to every one of those youth?"

Tears began to drip from his eyes. "God said, 'I love you'! What else would God say to a young person trying to follow him?"

You can probably figure out my point. We have emphasized that God wants us to evangelize so much that many missionaries are sent by manipulation, guilt, or misplaced ambition rather than by God. Thus, they are ill-equipped to face the crushing failures that even successful and famous missionaries often face at the outset of their mission.

Evangelism is not the only good work. Instead, the first and best evangelism is doing good to others (Matt. 5:13-16; 1 Thess. 1:6-10), even others who are of the household of faith (Gal. 6:10). Jesus said, "By this everyone will know that you are my disciples, if you have love for one another" (Jn. 13:35). This is the only call most Christians have to evangelism, to love one another and to do good to everyone.

When we get our foundations right, our people will grow, and God will send those who are ready for the battle that is missions work. In the meantime, as we love one another, we will be such a great light that we will be like a city on a hill that cannot be hidden (Matt. 5:13-16). We will reach the world if we use the methods the Bible teaches us to use.

In the middle of the second century, one Christian was trying to describe Christianity to the emperor. His description of the spread of Christianity is interesting:

> He has exhorted us to lead all men, by patience and gentleness, from shame and the love of evil. And this indeed is proved in the case of many who once were of your way of thinking, but have changed their violent and tyrannical disposition, being overcome either by the constancy which they have witnessed in their neighbors' lives, or by the extraordinary forbearance they have observed in their fellow travelers when defrauded, or by the honesty of those with whom they have transacted business.[34]

Justin Martyr listed three ways that Romans were converted by the Church. All three of them involve the remarkable lives of the Christians rather than verbal evangelism.

There were evangelists and missionaries in the second century, of course. Justin himself traveled around in philosopher's robes preaching the Gospel to anyone who would ask about his philosophy. Irenaeus, one of the most famous bishops of the second century, traveled from Smyrna in modern Turkey to Gaul in modern France to help spread the Gospel among the barbarian tribes. The early Christians knew, however, that selfless lives, lived out by people who loved each other, would shine a light that their neighbors could not ignore. As a result, their neighbors asked a reason for the hope that was in them, and they were prepared to answer (1 Pet. 3:15).

---

[34] Justin Martyr, c. 155-165, *First Apology*, ch. 16

The effect was astounding. Another early Christian, an African lawyer named Tertullian, described the powerful effect of love between Christians. He wrote:

> It is mainly the deeds of a love so noble that lead many to put a brand upon us. "See," they say, "how [the Christians] love one another," for they themselves [the Romans] are animated by mutual hatred. "How they are ready even to die for one another," for they themselves will sooner put to death. And they are angry with us, too, because we call each other brethren; for no other reason, as I think, than because among themselves names of consanguinity [i.e., blood relation] are assumed in mere pretense of affection.[35]

Let me translate that paragraph into modern English. Even when Romans were in the same family, they did not love each other the way Christians did. As a result, they marveled at the love of the Christians that was so great they were willing to die for one another.

How effective was this Christian love? Tertullian is the same author who famously said, "The blood of Christians is seed." Right before that, he writes, "The more of us you mow down, the more of us there are."[36] He gives us an idea of just how "more in number" they had grown:

> Without arms even, and raising no insurrectionary banner, but simply in enmity to you, we [Christians] could carry on the contest with you by an ill-willed severance alone. For if such multitudes of men were to break away from you and betake themselves to some remote corner of the world, why, the very loss of so many citizens, whatever sort they were, would cover the empire with shame, nay, in the very forsaking, vengeance would be inflicted. Why, you would be horror-struck at the solitude in which you would find yourselves, at such an all-prevailing silence ... You would have to seek subjects to govern. You would have more enemies than citizens remaining. For now it is the immense number of Christians which makes

---

[35] Tertullian, c. 197-220, *Apology*, ch. 39; brackets mine
[36] Tertullian. c. 197-220, *Apology*, ch. 50

your enemies so few, almost all the inhabitants of your various cities being followers of Christ.[37]

Most scholars would consider this paragraph highly exaggerated (as would I). The Christians were certainly not the majority of the Roman Empire nor its major cities until Constantine the Great rose to power in the early fourth century. Nonetheless, Tertullian could not have made such a claim without some basis in fact.

Jesus said that if we loved one another, the world would know that we are his disciples (Jn. 13:35). Later he prayed for us to be one because this would prove to the world that the Father sent him (Jn. 17:20-23). The early Christians did this, and their love and unity powerfully convinced the world that they were sent by Jesus and that Jesus was the Son of God with power to change lives.

The divine plan for the churches to "arise and shine" (Isa. 60:1) by displaying good works to glorify the Father and enlighten the world (Matt. 5:14-16), was very effective. Admittedly, this was in addition to those missionaries and evangelists who were sent (Rom. 10:15), but notice Justin's and Tertullian's focus. It was not on missionaries, but on the love of Christians for one another and their kindness to those outside. Paul was able to give the same testimony of the Thessalonians in the first century (1 Thess. 1:6-8).

Paul's letters to the churches indicate that our focus should be like theirs. His letters are full of advice on adhering to Christ, walking by the Spirit, turning away from iniquity, and doing good works, but they barely touch on evangelism. While we proclaim today that Christianity is not a religion of dos and don'ts, Paul filled the last half of every letter with dos and don'ts. He cared so much for good works, that he commanded Titus not to let anyone stop him from speaking continually on the subject:

> [Jesus] gave himself for us, that he might redeem us from all iniquity and purify for himself his own special people, zealous for good works. Say these things and exhort and reprove with all authority. Let no one despise you. (Tit. 2:14-15)

And:

---

[37] Tertullian, c. 197-220, *Apology*, ch. 37

> This saying is faithful, and concerning these things I desire that you affirm confidently, so that those who believe in God may be careful to maintain good works. (Tit. 3:8).

In modern churches, we want to invite our neighbors into our church meetings so that we can convert them with talk, whether from the pulpit or from discussions in Sunday School. As a result, our church meetings are geared as much for outsiders and nominal Christians as they are for the truly committed church members. But what has been the result of that method? It is possible that American Christianity, as a whole, is as much or more a testimony *against* Christ than a testimony *for* him. Jesus prayed that we would be one *so that* the world would know that the Father sent him. American Christianity, rather than being known for unity, is infamous for the opposite!

In such an environment. it is no wonder our main picture of evangelism is talking. We have no unity, we do not promote good works the way Paul told us to (Tit. 2:14-15; 3:8), and thus we have no shining city on a hill. Instead, we are limited to "this little light of mine."

Happily, there are notable exceptions, both individually and corporately. More and more churches are beginning to realize the desperate need to disciple their members. A discipleship conference I attended in Nashville in 2017 drew over a thousand attendees. Sixteen organizations were there to present their various plans for discipling churches by discipling individuals. This was very encouraging to see.

It is also extremely important. If we do not raise up disciples in our churches, then whom are we sending out as missionaries and evangelists? Missionaries will reproduce the kind of Christianity in which they grew up spiritually.

This can be seen in the results. It is a common saying in west Africa that African Christianity is "a mile wide and an inch deep." I have heard this from several missionaries, but the most telling source of that saying was the mayor of Gulu, Uganda! I was in Gulu to visit a mission there, and somehow we wound up at a civil function. The mayor was talking about ending corruption, and he wanted help from the churches, but they needed cleaning up as much as the government did!

It is the Bible that teaches us to equip the people of God to do good works and to love one another. This equipping is tied directly to evangelism and to reaching the world. We have seen that evangelism is among the good works the Scriptures, grace, the atonement, and the Spirit equip us to do, but it is not "the" work that we are equipped to do.

What Good Works Are

We have already begun to cover what good works are. The greatest of these is to love one another. But let us look at some specific ways to love another and to do good to those outside the household of faith.

We have several sources from which to find the good works that we are created in Christ Jesus to do. There are commands in every letter Paul wrote. There are things to avoid, and there are things to do (e.g., Rom. 11:9-12:1; Eph. 4:20-32). Many powerful church movements, blessed by God, have made the Sermon on the Mount (Matt. 5-7) their guide for living. I would argue that the best description of good works in the Bible is the Sermon on the Mount.

If God meant Psalm 119, which devotes 176 verses to praising God's words, commands, and decrees, to have any permanent influence among his people, then taking the time to learn the commands and teachings of God is central to our lives as Jesus' disciples. Peter told us to add virtue to our faith, but the first thing to add to our virtue is knowledge (2 Pet. 1:5). We come to Christ with some knowledge, whether from our culture, our parents, or our consciences, of what is virtuous, and Peter told us that the first thing we should do once we have faith is live virtuously. The next step, though, is to refine that virtue—those good works—by gaining knowledge. That knowledge comes from the Scriptures (2 Tim. 3:14-17), from the Spirit of God (Rom. 8:3-4, 13-14; Gal. 5:16-24), from our church leaders (Eph. 4:11-16; 1 Thes. 5:12-13; Heb. 13:17), and from one another (Heb. 3:13; 10:24-25).

Simply put, to learn to do good works is to learn to do the commands of Christ. This does not mean simply learning rules; it requires the power of the Spirit to be a doer of good works. Apart from Jesus, we can do nothing (Jn. 15:5). To be a Christian is to be led by the Spirit (Rom. 8:9,14). Nonetheless, the New Testament is packed with commands, and Jesus said that the only ones who love him are the ones who obey him (Jn. 14:21).

Again, as described in chapter four, we need the Scriptures, grace, the Holy Spirit, and the exhortation of our brothers and sisters to live obedient Christian lives. We have also seen, in the same chapter, that neither Jesus nor his apostles were talking about sinless perfection. Nonetheless, if our lives do not show a pattern of obeying his commands, we neither know him (1 Jn. 2:3-4) nor love him (Jn. 14:21), and we are not his friends (Jn. 15:14).

Of course, we know that Jesus put two commands above all the others, adding that the Law and Prophets depend on those commands (Matt. 22:40). Paul says love is the fulfillment of the Law (Rom. 13:10). The apostle John, despite all the frightening statements that are in his first letter, wraps them all up in love as well (1 Jn. 4:7-8). He uses "love" 23 times in the 105 verses of his first epistle.

I am summing up good works here as loving one another, loving others, and obeying Jesus' commands. Those early Christians—the ones that reached so many Romans by their good works that Tertullian claimed that if they left, the emperors would have no one left to rule over—made plenty of references to New Testament commands such as this passage from Polycarp:

> He who raised [Jesus] up from the dead will raise up us also, if we do His will, and walk in His commandments, and love what He loved, keeping ourselves from all unrighteousness, covetousness, love of money, evil speaking, false witness; not rendering evil for evil, or railing for railing, or blow for blow, or cursing for cursing, but being mindful of what the Lord said in His teaching: "Judge not, that ye be not judged"; "forgive, and it shall be forgiven unto you"; "be merciful, that ye may obtain mercy"; "with what measure ye mete, it shall be measured to you again;" and once more, "Blessed are the poor,

and those that are persecuted for righteousness' sake, for theirs is the kingdom of God."[38]

I could produce many lists of commands like this one, but it is best to get them directly from Jesus and his apostles. At the end of the Sermon on the Mount, which has most of the commands Polycarp listed, Jesus said:

> Everyone therefore who hears these words of mine and does them, I will liken him to a wise man who built his house on a rock. The rain came down, the floods came, and the winds blew and beat on that house; and it didn't fall, for it was founded on the rock. (Matt. 7:23-24)

This is an important and powerful promise! Jesus told us that if we will do the things that are in the Sermon on the Mount, then we will build our lives on the Rock, and the troubles of this life will not cause us to fall! Again, the premise of the New Testament is that we need the power of the Holy Spirit to obey Jesus' teachings. Setting our mind on spiritual things is foundational to New Testament living (Rom. 8:1-8). If we are Christians, though, we have the Spirit (Rom. 8:9), and thus we can be inheritors of this great promise. It is very similar to what Peter promises if we will add virtue, knowledge, self-control, perseverance, godliness, brotherly kindness, and love to our faith. He promises that if those things are growing in us, we will never be "idle or unfruitful" in the knowledge of our Lord Jesus.

It is well worth reading first the Sermon on the Mount, then all the New Testament to learn the commands of Jesus. Our goal is eternal life! Our Master asks us to lose our souls so that we can save them! Our Father calls us to love him "with all your heart, and with all your soul, and with all your mind, and with all your strength" (Mark 12:30)! It is worth being like David delighting yourself in the statutes of the Lord (Ps. 119:16).

Finally, I want to put one brand of good works in a special class. James, the Lord's brother, wrote, "Pure religion and undefiled before our God and Father is this: to visit the fatherless and widows in their affliction, and to keep oneself unstained by the

---

[38] Polycarp, c. 110-140, "Epistle to the Philippians," ch. 2

world" (1:27). James included "unstained by the world," which, in a sense, covers all the commands we are given, including walking by the Spirit. He singles out, though, taking care of orphans and widows.

This seems to be a general focus of Scripture as well. God takes 14 verses to complain about the disobedience of Israel through Isaiah (Isaiah 2-15), but when he tells them what to obey, his list is short:

> Learn to do well. Seek justice. Relieve the oppressed. Defend the fatherless. Plead for the widow. (Isaiah 1:17)

Jesus seems to agree. When he describes the final judgment, he focuses on a narrow category of works. Those who enter eternal life in the Kingdom of Heaven (Matt. 25:34,46) are those who fed the hungry, gave drink to the thirsty, took in strangers, clothed the naked, and visited the sick and imprisoned (vv. 35-36). Those who go into everlasting fiery punishment (vv. 41,46), are those who did not do those things (vv. 43-44).

Surely the emphasis put on these types of good works by Jesus and his half-brother James indicates that they are acts of love even more than other commands. Whether that is true or not, Jesus singled them out to represent the works for which we will be judged.

And since we are on the judgment, this is an excellent place to discuss just how Jesus prepares us for it.

7. Rebuilding the Atonement

During my first ten years as a Christian, I attended the Assembly of God, the Church of God in Christ, an Open Bible Church, two different Baptist churches and some independent churches, usually charismatic. Every one of those churches tried to drive home to me that works have nothing to do with eternal life.

Their efforts failed because one passage was eating away at me:

> [God] "will pay back to everyone according to their works:" to those who by patience in well-doing seek for glory, honor, and incorruptibility, [he will repay] eternal life. (Rom. 2:6-7, brackets mine)

When I asked about this passage in Romans, I was told that it was hypothetical. "If" we had the power to do good works, then we would be able to obtain eternal life by patience in well-doing. Since we do not have the power to do good works, I was told, there is a different method for receiving eternal life. It is given to us without judgment because Jesus died for our sins. While no one would dare use these words, what they conveyed to me was "since no one can do good works, Romans 2:6-7 can safely be dismissed."

I could not agree. Dismissing Scripture is never a good idea. I wrestled with Romans 2:6-7 and passages like it for years before I was able to come to an understanding of them.[39] Let's begin with the passage most similar to Romans 2:6-7.

Everyone seems to know Galatians 6:7-8:

> Do not be deceived: God cannot be mocked. A man reaps what he sows. Whoever sows to please their flesh, from the flesh will reap destruction; whoever sows to please the Spirit, from the Spirit will reap eternal life.

---

[39] I do not know if I would ever have caught the simple key to faith and works in the writings of the apostle Paul if I had not been introduced to the early church fathers. Among other things, one line in the "Epistle to Diognetus" was key. It says, "... having made it manifest that in ourselves we were unable to enter into the kingdom of God, we might through the power of God be made able" (Anonymous, c. 130-200, "Epistle to Diognetus," ch. 9). Hopefully, the rest of this chapter will bring out the importance of that statement.

A lot of people also at least recognize Galatians 6:9:

> Let us not become weary in doing good, for at the proper time we will reap a harvest if we do not give up.

We seem to know both passages, but we do not combine them. If we did, then we would have to answer this question: what harvest will we reap if we do not grow weary in doing good and if we do not give up?

Since verse 9 is in the context of verses 7 and 8, we must answer that we will reap eternal life, but only if we do not grow weary in doing good. And yes, we rely on the Holy Spirit to keep doing good without giving up. Nonetheless, if we want to reap eternal life, we must not become weary in doing good.

It should be obvious that choosing to ignore or dismiss a Scripture passage, especially in Romans, is not a good idea. In this case it is an especially bad idea. Romans 2:6-7 is practically repeated in a passage we do not dismiss: Galatians 6:7-9.

Romans 2:6-7 does not specifically mention that apart from Christ we can do nothing (Jn. 15:5), nor does it mention that in the flesh we cannot please God (Rom. 8:8). The passage does not mention that to patiently do good, we must be born again, obtain grace, be filled with the Holy Spirit, and use the Scriptures to thoroughly equip one another to do good works.[40] Galatians 6:8-9, however, does imply all this. There we are told that by sowing to the Spirit, we can avoid "growing weary in doing good." If we avoid growing weary in doing good, then, obviously, we can patiently continue to do good and reap eternal life.

This relationship between Romans 2:6-7 and Galatians 6:7-9 provides a perfect opportunity to explain why evangelicals get so confused about faith, works, and the atonement.

Romans 2:6-7 gives us a formula in which all of us agree there is a problem. The formula is:

1. Pursue glory, honor, and immortality by patiently doing good works throughout our life.
2. God will repay us for our works

---

[40] See chapter four.

3. We receive eternal life.

We all agree that the problem inherent in this passage is that humans, in general, are unable to patiently continue in good works. We all also agree that Jesus solved the problem by his death and resurrection.

Evangelicals believe that Jesus' death takes care of the judgment because his righteousness replaces, and thus excuses, our unrighteousness on judgment day. They further believe that because God's wrath was expended on Jesus, believers in Jesus will not face his wrath on judgment day.

Notice that the evangelical system requires no change in us. It is God's way of handling sin that is changed by Jesus' death. It might be said that under the evangelical system, Jesus died for God rather than for us.

The Bible, however, teaches that Jesus died to change us. He died for the *aphesis* of sins, the eradication of sin's power over us and the restoration of all our rights as children of God. As newborn children of God, no longer slaves to sin, the Holy Spirit, the fellowship of the saints, and the Scriptures all enable us to do good works. The problem of Romans 2:6-7, described above, is resolved by the new birth and vast resources from heaven that enable us to do good.

Standard evangelical tradition denies the possibility of obtaining eternal life by doing good and thus contradicts Romans 2:6-7. By contradicting Romans 2:6-7, evangelical tradition contradicts Galatians 6:7-9 as well.

This explains the handling of Galatians 6 that I experienced in a Baptist Sunday School class. The teacher read the three verses, then asked, "Does this mean you can lose your salvation?"

After some awkward silence, he chuckled, and said, "No, it doesn't." His nervous class corporately exhaled the breath they were holding.

Then, without any explanation at all, he moved on to verse 10.

That really happened; I am not making this up. I wrote him a letter saying, "Even if you don't believe those verses say we can lose our salvation, the passage is a warning. I think you should have passed on the warning to your class."

The letter was longer because he was a friend. I tried to make my exhortation as soft as I could. Nonetheless, he did not respond. Instead, he gave my letter to the pastor, and I was called in to explain why I felt free to correct one of "his" Sunday School teachers.

This happened long before I understood the things I am writing today. Without realizing it, I was touching a foundational doctrine, a cornerstone of evangelical tradition. In our songs and in our sermons, evangelicals testify that Jesus eliminated the judgment by works that is described in Romans 2:5-8. We are no longer required to patiently continue to do good, evangelicals teach, because Jesus died to pay the price for our sins. He took care of the Romans 2:6 judgment, we teach, by his blood.

There are two problems with this doctrine.

1. Even Christians are going to be judged by their works, both good and bad (2 Cor. 5:10; 1 Pet. 1:17).
2. We are still threatened with punishment for our sins, and that punishment sounds a lot like not being condemned with the world (Gal. 5:19-21; 6:7; Eph. 5:5-7; 2 Pet. 2:20-21; Rev. 3:4-5).

If Jesus' death eliminated the judgment according to works, then why will the bad things we did come up at the judgment? (2 Cor. 5:10). Why will a Christian who lives in the flesh reap corruption (Gal. 6:7), die (Rom. 8:12), and be unable to inherit the Kingdom of God (Gal. 5:19-21)? Why will those who "escaped the defilement of the world through the knowledge of the Lord and Savior Jesus Christ" be worse off than before they were saved if they "are again entangled in it and overcome"? (2 Pet. 2:20). Why will only the undefiled members of the church in Sardis walk with Jesus in white? (Rev. 3:4-5).

The answer to these questions is that Jesus did not die to eliminate or change the judgment. The judgment was already just. God did not need to change. He was already merciful. Jesus did not die to change God nor to change the way God judges. Jesus died to change us. He died to free us from slavery to sin.

This is why Paul wrote:

> Much more then, being now justified by his blood, we will be saved from God's wrath through him. For if while we were enemies, we were reconciled to God through the death of his Son, much more, being reconciled, we will be saved by his life. (Rom. 5:9-10).

Notice that we are not yet saved from God's wrath. We "will be" saved from God's wrath. This is worth unpacking.

In Ephesians 5:5, Paul warns Christians that:

> ... no sexually immoral person, nor unclean person, nor covetous man, who is an idolater, has any inheritance in the Kingdom of Christ and God.

This is followed immediately, by:

> ... because of these things, the wrath of God comes on the children of disobedience. Therefore don't be partakers with them.

The point here is obvious. If we are sexually immoral, unclean, and covetous, we will not receive what obedient Christians receive, an inheritance in God's kingdom; instead, the wrath of God will come upon us because we made ourselves partners with the sons of disobedience.

Therefore, Paul says we "will be" saved from God's wrath through Jesus (Rom. 5:9). In the next verse, he specifies that we will be saved "by his life." This is a reference to the Christian life as described in Galatians 2:20:

> I have been crucified with Christ, and it is no longer I who live, but Christ lives in me. That life which I now live in the flesh, I live by faith in the Son of God, who loved me, and gave himself up for me.

Yes, Paul is describing himself in that passage, but in the same letter, he writes, "Those who belong to Christ have crucified the flesh with its passions and lusts" (Gal. 5:24). Paul did not believe himself to be different from other Christians. He wrote, "Be imitators of me, even as I also am of Christ" (1 Cor. 11:1).

Jesus did die to save us from God's wrath, but not in the way we are normally taught. Jesus did not change the entire system of

God's judgment. It remains true that "it is appointed to men to die once, and after this, judgment" (Heb. 9:27). Now, though, we can be prepared to face it.

The "Favor" of Eternal Life

Romans 6:22 is an excellent summation of all that I have written in this book. It says:

> But now, being made free from sin and having become servants of God, you have your fruit of sanctification and the result of eternal life.

Short and simple: God freed us from sin, giving ourselves to his service yielded the fruit of sanctification, and the result of sanctification is eternal life; wonderful and clear confirmation of all I have written.

But what of the next verse, Romans 6:23?

> For the wages of sin is death, but the free gift of God is eternal life in Christ Jesus our Lord. (Rom. 6:23)

If, as the WEB translation of Romans 6:23 states, eternal life is the "free" gift of God, then everything I have written in this book is false, and Paul contradicted himself. In Romans 2:6-7, he told us that eternal life is a reward or repayment. The Greek verb used in Romans 2:6 is used "esp. of wages, debts, oaths, etc."[41] In other words, the gift of eternal life in Romans 2:6 is not free, but a repayment for patiently doing good.

If eternal life is a "free" gift of God, then Paul is even contradicting the previous verse, in which eternal life is the "result" of sanctification.

My point, of course, is that eternal life is not a "free" gift. It is a gift, but not an unconditional one. We have spent the whole book looking at the one condition that God requires before he gives eternal life: good works.

The Greek word for gift in Romans 6:23 is *charisma*. A run through the lexicons at StudyBible.info gives the reason that some translations choose to add "free" to "gift" when translating

---

[41] GreekLexicon.org, 2012-2018, "591: ἀποδίδωμι"

charisma. You will find the words "grace" and "favor" peppered throughout the suggested translations of *charisma*. This is because the Greek word for "grace" is *charis*. Thus, a *charisma* is a gift founded in *charis*, in favor. It need not be free to be a *charisma*, but it must be a favor, a gift given out of a favorable attitude toward the recipient of the gift. Thus, *charisma* should not be translated as a "free" gift but, as *A Greek Lexicon* by Liddell and Scott suggests, a "favour bestowed." Liddell and Scott's lexicon does not include "free" in any suggested definition of *charisma*.[42]

"What is the difference?" you might ask. If you can bear with me through this point, you will love this thought. Whether you are convinced by what I am teaching in this book or not, you will love this point.

In Romans 4, written in passing so that it is easily overlooked, Paul explains exactly what makes grace to be grace. In fact, "favor" is a much better translation of *charis* than "grace" is, so Paul is explaining just what makes a favor a favor:

> Now to him who works, the reward is not counted as grace, but as something owed. (Rom. 4:4)

In other words, if I hire an employee at $10 per hour and he works 40 hours in a week, I am not doing him a favor by paying him $400. I am giving him something I owe him.

Paul says something similar in Romans 11:6:

> And if by grace, then it is no longer of works; otherwise grace is no longer grace. But if it is of works, it is no longer grace; otherwise work is no longer work.

Again, Paul is putting work and works together. If someone received something as a favor (grace), then it was not wages. If it were wages in return for work, then it cannot be a favor.

Thus, after everything I have written in this book, we must conclude, based on Romans 6:23, that eternal life cannot be earned wages for doing good. Even though God only rewards eternal life to those who patiently continue to do good, and even though Romans 2:6-7 calls it a "repayment," he does not consider it a

---

[42] Liddell & Scott, 1940, *A Greek-English Lexicon*, "χαῖρ-ισμα , ατος, τό,"

wage, something earned, but a favor, something given. No matter how much good we do, we cannot *earn* eternal life. It is not something we deserve, but something God gives to those in his favor.

Many centuries ago, a Christian teacher dubbed "Golden Tongue" by his peers wrote the following of Romans 6:23:

> After speaking of the wages of sin, in the case of the blessings, he has not kept to the same order: for he does not say, "the wages of good deeds," but "the gift of God"; to show, *that it was not of themselves that they were freed*, nor was it a due they received, neither yet a return, nor a recompense of labors, but by grace all these things came about.[43]

John Chrysostom (Greek for "Golden Tongue") understood what all Christians of his time understood, that to be freed from sin and called to holiness was a great gift to be rejoiced over and treasured. To receive the "precious and exceedingly great promises" and thus to have "escaped from the corruption that is in the world by lust" (2 Pet. 1:4) is a gift of favor already, even if it were not *also* rewarded with eternal life!

Chrysostom explains further in his comments on Romans 6:22

> For to prevent your saying everything lies in hope, he points out that you have already reaped fruits, first the being freed from wickedness ...; second, the being made a servant unto righteousness; a third, the enjoying of holiness; a fourth, the obtaining of life, and life too not for a season, but everlasting.[44]

He explains that in order to prevent us from complaining that all our rewards are in the future ("lie in hope"), Paul points out that we have already received the gifts of being freed from wickedness, being made a servant to righteousness, enjoying a life of holiness and, on top of all those gifts, the additional gift of having the life of God in us which will last forever!

Eternal life cannot be a wage for our good works because our good works were already a gift of grace, a "favor bestowed"! God has favored us with those "precious and exceeding great promises"

---

[43] Chrysostom, d. 407, "Homilies on Romans," Homily 12; emphasis mine
[44] Chrysostom, d. 407, "Homilies on Romans," Homily 12

so that we would not drown in the mire, unhappiness, hopelessness, and desperation caused by "the corruption that is in the world by lust"!

Perhaps the worst fruit that Calvinism has produced is the idea that good works are a heavy burden. Jesus told us that the one he sets free "will be free indeed" (Jn. 8:36). He said his yoke is easy and his burden light (Matt. 11:30). Receiving the Holy Spirit and keeping Jesus' commands is a great gift that produces "righteousness, peace, and joy in the Holy Spirit" (Rom. 14:17). We are not laboring like slaves to obtain an almost unobtainable gift. Instead:

> Being ... justified by faith, we have peace with God through our Lord Jesus Christ; through whom we also have our access by faith into this grace [favor] in which we stand. We rejoice in hope of the glory of God. Not only this, but we also rejoice in our sufferings, knowing that suffering produces perseverance; and perseverance, proven character; and proven character, hope: and hope doesn't disappoint us, because God's love has been poured into our hearts through the Holy Spirit who was given to us. For while we were yet weak, at the right time Christ died for the ungodly. (Rom. 5:1-6)

To be able to celebrate in suffering is a gift from heaven. Christians are free; they can rejoice at all times because by the Spirit, they have crucified the flesh with its lusts that used to keep us in bondage. This is not the great requirement of faith; this is the great gift of faith, that we can be free through Jesus Christ from the corruption that is in the world through lust!

Chrysostom continued regarding Romans 6:23:

> And so there was a superiority for this cause also, in that He did not free them only, or change their condition for a better, but that He did it without any labor or trouble upon their part: and that He not only freed them, but also gave them much more than before, and that through His Son.[45]

There is an ancient story that also expresses this idea. Long in the past, probable somewhere around A.D. 160, a man named

---

[45] Chrysostom, d. 407, "Homilies on Romans," Homily 12

Hermas wrote a book now called *The Shepherd of Hermas*)or *The Pastor of Hermas*). In it, an "Angel of Repentance" appeared to him to teach him. The story consists of three books: one of visions, one of commandments, and one of similes. The book of commandments contains twelve commandments and, at the end, Hermas asks:

> Sir, these commandments are great, and good, and glorious, and fitted to gladden the heart of the man who can perform them. But I do not know if these commandments can be kept by man, because they are exceeding hard.[46]

The angel told him, "If you lay it down as certain that they can be kept, then you will easily keep them, and they will not be hard," but it was clear he was angry. Hermas was frightened, and when the angel saw Hermas "agitated and confused," he told him gently:

> O fool, senseless and doubting, do you not perceive how great is the glory of God, and how strong and marvellous, in that He created the world for the sake of man, and subjected all creation to him, and gave him power to rule over everything under heaven? If, then, man is lord of the creatures of God, and rules over all, is he not able to be lord also of these commandments? For ... the man who has the Lord in his heart can also be lord of all, and of every one of these commandments. But to those who have the Lord only on their lips, but their hearts hardened, and who are far from the Lord, the commandments are hard and difficult. Put, therefore, ye who are empty and fickle in your faith, the Lord in your heart, and ye will know that there is nothing easier or sweeter, or more manageable, than these commandments.[47]

Imagine what it might be like if we were to restore this understanding of Jesus' commandments. That we would believe not only that Jesus' commandments are easy and light, as he taught (Matt. 11:30), but that they are easy, sweet, and manageable. Then we might be like David, the king and psalmist, who considered even Moses' commandments to be "sweet[er] ... than honey to my mouth" (Ps. 119:103) and who ran "in the path of [God's]

---

[46] Hermas, c. 160, *The Pastor of Hermas*, Commandment Twelfth, ch. 3
[47] Hermas, c. 160, *The Pastor of Hermas*, Commandment Twelfth, ch. 4

commandments" because his heart was set free (Ps. 119:32). With such an attitude, following the life-giving commands of Christ, who is far greater than Moses, we can "rejoice greatly with joy that is unspeakable and full of glory, receiving the result of [our] faith, the salvation of [our] souls" (1 Pet. 1:8).

Old Testament Sacrifices

This chapter may not have sounded much like an exposition of the atonement. I have not addressed Old Testament sacrifices and how these typify the sacrifice of God's Son. I have not addressed the incredible prophecy of the sacrifice of the Messiah in Isaiah 53. This is because evangelicals have those things right. The Old Testament sacrifices do typify his sacrifice for sin. Jesus did take our sins upon him as Isaiah 53 prophesied. No correction is needed there.

Instead, I have focused on one thing: Jesus did not die to give Christians a free pass at the judgment. His death did not change the judgment; it was already just. It did not make God more willing to forgive our sins; he already "freely" pardoned sins (Isa. 55:7), and his mercy already endured forever. He died to set us free from sin.

I do, however, want to touch on two things: what animal sacrifice was *not* for, and the New Testament Scriptures on what Jesus did die for.

One of the most surprising things I found when I began reading the early church fathers was their view of animal sacrifices. We evangelicals teach that animal sacrifices stopped because once Jesus died, they were unnecessary. The early church fathers taught that God never wanted animal sacrifices.

I suspect that your initial reaction to this idea, like mine, is that it is ridiculous. Leviticus is packed full of instructions about animal sacrifice. How could God possibly not want them?

Let's begin by discussing who the early church fathers are. When evangelicals hear "early church fathers," the names that usually come to mind are men like Augustine and Jerome, neither of which is "early," by my definition. The majority of both men's ministry was in the 400s, the fifth century.

When I speak of the early church fathers, I am speaking of men like Clement of Rome, an elder in the church of Rome who wrote a letter on their behalf to the church of Corinth in the *first century*. I think of Justin Martyr, who gave the earliest full description of a Sunday morning church service around A.D. 155 or 160. I think of Irenaeus, a missionary to the barbarians, who wrote a five-volume apology for the Christian faith in the 180s.

These men wrote during a time when the churches across the known world were in unity and communion with one another. Their basic doctrines were agreed upon around the world. This agreement was the result of the teaching of the apostles in the churches they founded, not a result of some central authority that decreed dogma. There was no such central authority.[48] Across the board and in agreement, the early church fathers of the second and third centuries teach that God never wanted animal sacrifices. Justin Martyr explains:

> Under [Moses] your nation [i.e., the Jews] appeared unrighteous and ungrateful to God, making a calf in the wilderness. Therefore, God accommodated himself to that nation and commanded them to offer sacrifices, as if to his name, so that you would not serve idols.[49]

When Justin wrote to Roman emperors, he says it is "tradition" that taught him "God does not need the material offerings which men can give."[50] Speaking to the Jews, however, he quotes Scripture:

> "And that you may learn that it was for the sins of your own nation and for their idolatries and not because there was any necessity for such sacrifices, that they were likewise enjoined, listen to the manner in which he speaks of these by Amos, one of the twelve [minor prophets], saying: '... I have hated, I have

---

[48] Many Roman Catholics, and even *The Catechism of the Catholic Church*, would contest my claim that there was no central authority for the churches worldwide in the second century. They are the only ones who would, and even the Roman Catholic Church has been backing off that claim during meetings with leaders of the Lutherans and Orthodox. I document all this in *Rome's Audacious Claim*, published in 2019.

[49] Justin Martyr, c. 155-165, *Dialogue with Trypho*, ch. 19

[50] Justin Martyr, c. 155-165, *First Apology*, ch. 10

> despised your feast-days, and I will not smell in your solemn assemblies. Therefore, though you offer me your burnt-offerings and sacrifices, I will not accept them; neither will I regard the peace-offerings of your presence. ... But let judgment be rolled down as water, and righteousness as an impassable torrent [Amos 5:21-22,24].[51]

Rather than deluge you with quotes from other Christians of the second and third century, quotes you can find on my web site,[52] I want to show you the verses they quote from the Old Testament, most of which you have probably never noticed nor considered. Jeremiah 7:21-23 is the most shocking of these verses, and it is often cited by the earliest Christians.

> The Lord of Armies, the God of Israel says: "Add your burnt offerings to your sacrifices and eat meat. For I didn't speak to your fathers or command them in the day that I brought them out of the land of Egypt concerning burnt offerings or sacrifices; but this thing I commanded them, saying, 'Listen to my voice, and I will be your God, and you shall be my people. Walk in all the way that I command you, that it may be well with you.'"

Justin's explanation, above, is the perfect explanation of God's shocking statement through Jeremiah. God made sacrifices a requirement only after Israel made the golden calf.

We have already seen Justin's quote from Amos. Such quotes are common throughout the major and minor prophets. Hosea 6:6, for example says:

> For I desire mercy, and not sacrifice; and the knowledge of God more than burnt offerings.

I suspect most evangelicals have sung the song from Micah 6:8:

> He has shown thee, o man, what is good and what the Lord requires of thee: but to do justly, and to love mercy, and to walk humbly with thy God.

---

[51] Justin Martyr, c. 155-165, *Dialogue with Trypho*, ch. 22
[52] Pavao, 2009-2021, "Quotes about Sacrifices"

What you may not know is what precedes Micah 6:8:

> How shall I come before the Lord, and bow myself before the exalted God? Shall I come before him with burnt offerings, with calves a year old? Will the Lord be pleased with thousands of rams? With tens of thousands of rivers of oil? Shall I give my firstborn for my disobedience? The fruit of my body for the sin of my soul? (Micah 6:6-7)

No, none of these things. The Lord desires obedience rather than sacrifice (1 Sam. 15:22). He wants you to do justice, love mercy, and walk humbly with him (Micah 6:8).

The question to ask, then, is: "If the Lord desires obedience rather than sacrifice, then why was Jesus sacrificed?"

The answer to that is: "So that we could obey." This answer fits New Testament teaching so well that we can easily assemble New Testament passages that teach it without explanation:

> To this end Christ died, rose, and lived again, that he might be Lord of both the dead and the living. (Rom. 14:9)

> He died for all, that those who live should no longer live to themselves, but to him who for their sakes died and rose again. (2 Cor. 5:15)

> [Jesus] gave himself for us, that he might redeem us from all iniquity, and purify for himself a people for his own possession, zealous for good works. (Tit. 2:14)

> "Not everyone who says to me, 'Lord, Lord,' will enter into the Kingdom of Heaven, but he who does the will of my Father who is in heaven. Many will tell me in that day, 'Lord, Lord, didn't we prophesy in your name, in your name cast out demons, and in your name do many mighty works?' Then I will tell them, 'I never knew you. Depart from me, you who work iniquity.' Everyone therefore who hears these words of mine and does them, I will liken him to a wise man who built his house on a rock. The rain came down, the floods came, and the winds blew and beat on that house; and it didn't fall, for it was founded on the rock." (Jn. 7:21-25)

> For all have sinned and fall short of the glory of God. (Rom. 3:23)

For the good which I desire, I don't do; but the evil which I don't desire, that I practice. (Rom. 7:19)

For the law of the Spirit of life in Christ Jesus made me free from the law of sin and of death. For what the law couldn't do, in that it was weak through the flesh, God did, sending his own Son in the likeness of sinful flesh and for sin, he condemned sin in the flesh; that the ordinance of the law might be fulfilled in us, who walk not after the flesh, but after the Spirit. (Rom. 8:2-4)

You were made alive when you were dead in transgressions and sins, in which you once walked according to the course of this world, according to the prince of the power of the air, the spirit who now works in the children of disobedience. We also all once lived among them in the lusts of our flesh, doing the desires of the flesh and of the mind, and were by nature children of wrath, even as the rest. But God, being rich in mercy, for his great love with which he loved us, even when we were dead through our trespasses, made us alive together with Christ—by grace you have been saved. (Eph. 2:1-5)

For by grace you have been saved through faith, and that not of yourselves; it is the gift of God, not of works, that no one would boast. For we are his workmanship, created in Christ Jesus for good works, which God prepared before that we would walk in them. (Eph. 2:8-10)

For sin will not have dominion over you. For you are not under law, but under grace. (Rom. 6:14)

For the grace of God has appeared, bringing salvation to all men, instructing us to the intent that, denying ungodliness and worldly lusts, we would live soberly, righteously, and godly in this present age. (Tit. 2:11-12)

For as through the one man's disobedience many were made sinners, even so through the obedience of the one, many will be made righteous. (Rom. 5:19)

Our old man was crucified with him, that the body of sin might be done away with, so that we would no longer be in bondage

> to sin. For he who has died has been freed from sin. (Rom. 6:6-7)
>
> But now, being made free from sin and having become servants of God, you have your fruit of sanctification and the result of eternal life. (Rom. 6:22)
>
> His divine power has granted to us all things that pertain to life and godliness, through the knowledge of him who called us by his own glory and virtue, by which he has granted to us his precious and exceedingly great promises; that through these you may become partakers of the divine nature, having escaped from the corruption that is in the world by lust. (2 Pet. 1:3-4)

Those are the passages I could come up with off the top of my head. I am sure there are many more. To obey is better than sacrifice, but the sacrifice of Jesus was necessary so that we would obey and be among those who sow to the Spirit and do not grow weary in doing good (Rom. 8:2-4; Gal. 6:8-9).

Ephesians 1:7 & Colossians 1:14

I found this wonderful summation of the atonement only after I finished this book and thought it was ready for publication. I cannot leave this out. It is worth the late adjustment.

As we have seen, Jesus' blood did far more than forgive our sins. His blood purchased us (1 Cor. 6:19-20). He gave himself as a ransom (Matt. 20:28; 1 Tim. 2:6). He redeemed us with "precious blood" (1 Pet. 1:18-19).

"Redeemed" in 1 Peter 1:18, like "purchased" in 1 Corinthians 6:19-20 and "ransom" in Matthew 20:28, is a word that implies we were bought. The Greek word for "redeemed" in 1 Peter 1:18, *lutroo*, primarily means "to release upon receipt of ransom."[53]

With that information, let's look at Ephesians 1:7. If you are a Christian, this should thrill you, even take your breath away.

Ephesians 1:7 says:

---

[53] StudyBible.info. (n.d.). "G3084 λυτρόω - Strong's Greek Lexicon Number."

> ... in whom we have our redemption through his blood, the forgiveness of our trespasses, according to the riches of his grace ...

Colossians 1:14 says the same thing with fewer words. Both include the words "redemption" and *aphesis*, which means much more than "forgiveness," as we have seen throughout this book.

In Ephesians 1:7 and Colossians 1:14, "redemption" is *apolutrosis*, and the translations given at StudyBible.info include "a ransoming," "ransom in full," and "release effected by payment of ransom."

Combining *aphesis* and *apolutrosis* in Ephesians 1:7 and Colossians 1:14 give us a much better picture of what Jesus died for:

> In whom we have our "ransom in full" through his blood, the "release and restoration" from our trespasses, according to the riches of his grace.

The price and promise here are phenomenal. By his own blood, Jesus ransomed us, giving himself in our place, making us his own possession, releasing us from slavery to sin and all debt associated with it. It is a full ransom, rescuing us from sin's dominion, and translating us to "the kingdom of the Son of his love" (Col. 1:13).

No wonder Paul called it the "riches" of his favor. "Riches" almost seems an understatement.

This, of course, is not all there is to the atonement. What Jesus did on the cross and through the resurrection is too great for any of us to fully understand. The entire creation is groaning for the revelation of the sons of God! How awesome is that! I do not pretend to understand it, just to rejoice and stand in awe of it. I am trying only to provide the basic purpose of the atonement in a manner which correlates with God's just judgment, his overwhelming mercy and kindness, and the plain statements of Scripture.

With the rebuilding of the atonement, I have covered all the foundational topics I wanted to cover. I have not, however, sufficiently answered potential objections.

8. Salvation by Faith Alone and Other Objections

Salvation by Faith Alone

It is obvious, I assume, that if works have nothing to do with salvation, then the 40,000 words I have devoted to carefully rebuilding a biblical model of Christianity was a waste of my time and yours. The Bible suggests we might not have to worry about this possibility. That hint is James statement that "by works a man is justified, and not only by faith" (James 2:24). Surprisingly, this "not by faith alone" (NASB) is the only occurrence in the Bible of the term "faith alone"!

On the other hand, there are passages which seem to specifically contradict James. They tell us that salvation and justification are "apart from works" (Rom. 3:28) or "not of works" (Eph. 2:9).

> Where then is the boasting? It is excluded. By what kind of law? Of works? No, but by a law of faith. We maintain therefore that a man is justified by faith apart from the works of the law. (Rom. 3:28)

> For by grace you have been saved through faith, and that not of yourselves; it is the gift of God, not of works, that no one would boast. For we are his workmanship, created in Christ Jesus for good works, which God prepared before that we would walk in them. (Eph. 2:8-10)

We have already addressed this second passage, but only the part about being re-created in Christ Jesus to do good works. The first part, though, says we are saved by grace and not works. Further, both these passages say that salvation apart from works is what keeps us from boasting. How, then, can all the things I have been writing be true?

Of course, the corresponding question is also important. How can all the things we have looked at in the first seven chapters be false? We did not mishandle Scripture. We did not twist any verses. We simply read what they said and drew clear, logical conclusions from them. Now we are looking at verses that seem to contradict everything we have been learning.

Do not fault yourself for struggling with the contrast. Martin Luther thought James 2:24 ("not only by faith") and Romans 3:28 ("by faith apart from ... works") were impossible to reconcile. He offered his doctor's cap (the sign of his academic doctorate) to anyone who could reconcile them. All evangelicals struggle with this contrast.

This should be a warning that something is wrong. Before Martin Luther, there is no record of anyone struggling with the contrast. In fact, as I will show you shortly, early Christians regularly wrote in similar, seemingly contradictory terms.

The answer is simple, even obvious, though it is easily overlooked. I only found it because I began reading the early church fathers. One of the first letters I read contained the same sort of conflict we see in Paul and James.

The letter was from the bishop of the church in Smyrna to the church in Philippi, written sometime during the first half of the second century. The bishop of Smyrna at that time was Polycarp, whom scholars believe to have been appointed by the apostle John. He was later martyred for the faith. Outside the apostles, his credentials are as strong as anyone's.

In his letter, in the first paragraph, he wrote:

> ... in whom, though now you do not see him, you believe, and believing, rejoice with joy unspeakable and full of glory. Into this joy many desire to enter, knowing that by grace you are saved, not of works, but by the will of God through Jesus Christ.[54]

Clearly Polycarp understood and agreed with Ephesians 2:8-9. He both quoted it and said that it makes us "rejoice with joy unspeakable" (quoted from 1 Pet 1:8). But in the second paragraph, he wrote:

> He who raised [Jesus] up from the dead will raise up us also, if we do his will, walk in his commandments, love what he loved, keeping ourselves from all unrighteousness, covetousness, love

---

[54] Polycarp, c. 110-140, Epistle to the Philippians, ch. 1

of money, evil speaking, false witness, not rendering evil for evil, or railing for railing ...[55]

The first time I read this, I was very excited. While I still did not know why Paul could write Romans 3:28 and James could write James 2:24, I was certain that Polycarp did know. He wrote statements that seem to contradict in much the same way Paul and James did. Polycarp did not give the answer to this contradiction, but he obviously understood why they did not contradict. I was still puzzled, but I was also filled with hope.

Later, I ran across the anonymous letter to Diognetus, which was written about the same period. That letter contains this passage:

> As long then as the former time [i.e., the Old Testament] endured, [God] permitted us to be borne along by unruly impulses, being drawn away by the desire of pleasure and various lusts. This was not that he at all delighted in our sins, but that he simply endured them. Nor did he approve of the time of working iniquity that then was, but he sought to form a mind conscious of righteousness, so that being convinced in that time of our unworthiness of attaining life through our own works, it should now, through the kindness of God, be vouchsafed to us. And having made it manifest that in ourselves we were unable to enter the kingdom of God, we might through the power of God be made able.[56]

It was as I was reading this paragraph, not for the first time, that the answer struck me. Mind you, I had been mulling over Romans 2:5-8 and the judgment by works for about six years by then. It had been two years since I had first read Polycarp's letter. There was a lot of waiting, a lot of praying, and a lot of rejecting insufficient answers before God let me see something that is obvious once you realize it but, apparently, quite hidden when you do not.

---

[55] Polycarp, c. 110-140, Epistle to the Philippians, ch. 2
[56] Anonymous, c. 130-200, "Epistle to Diognetus," ch. 9; brackets mine

Romans 3:28 and the first chapter of Polycarp's letter are about the past.[57] We were (past tense) saved by faith apart from works. Polycarp's second chapter, saying that we will only be raised up if we do God's will, is in the future tense. The apostle Paul wrote the same thing about our future. Three times he tells us that those who practice sin will not inherit God's kingdom (1 Cor. 6:9-11; Gal. 5:19-21; Eph. 5:5).

This past/future distinction is consistent in Paul's letters. In the past tense he says we were saved apart from works, and in the future tense that we will receive, or not receive, eternal life because of our works.

I need to make a point here. This is not a theory. This is not a doctrine to be debated. It is an empirical fact that can be verified or falsified by simply reading Paul's letters.

In Paul's letters, we were (past tense) born again, saved, and brought to life in Christ by faith apart from works, so that no one can boast. In the future, on the last day, however, it is our works which will be judged. If we are immoral or unclean, or if we do not keep his commandments and do his will, we will not—future tense—be raised up with Christ, and we will not have any inheritance in his kingdom (Eph. 5:5 and Polycarp's "Epistle to the Philippians," ch. 2).

Let me pause to say again that I am speaking of a general pattern of righteousness, not sinless perfection. Paul warned the Galatians that those who "practice" (Gr. *prasso*) the works of the flesh will not inherit God's kingdom (Gal. 5:21). He is not warning the imperfect; he is warning those in danger of giving up or giving in.

---

[57] Someone pointed out to me that Romans 3:28 is not in the past tense, but the present. I missed that when I was writing this chapter because the passage is about our initial justification, when we first come to Christ. The whole verse reads, "We maintain therefore that a man is justified by faith apart from the works of the law." Paul is talking about how "a man"—any person—becomes a Christian. If he believes that Jesus is Lord, he will be justified—forgiven, freed from sin, born again, and filled with the Spirit—by faith and not works. That same man, like all other men, will face the judgment after he dies, and if he has not grown weary in doing good, he will reap eternal life.

The thing I saw in the Letter to Diognetus was that our problem is that we were—past tense—unable to enter the kingdom of God, and the solution God offered was to make us able. This helped me to see that Romans 2:5-8 was what we had to look forward to—future tense. If we want eternal life, we need to patiently do good works. The problem was that we were incapable of patiently doing good, so God made us capable.

Romans 8:1-4 explains how God did this. By Jesus' death, God takes all condemnation away (8:1), and we get to start over. God takes us out of "the law of sin and death" that Paul described in Romans 7, and he puts us under the "the law of the Spirit of life in Christ Jesus" (8:2). The Law could not stop us from doing what we do not want to do (7:15), but through the sacrifice of Jesus, God did what the Law could not do (8:3). Now, those who walk by the Spirit fulfill the righteous requirement of the Law (Rom. 8:3-4). So then, what was impossible for the natural or old covenant person in Romans 2:6 is simply normal life for those empowered by the Spirit.

This is true of all the passages in Paul's writings and Peter's. For example, in 2 Peter 1:3-11, verses 3 and 4 tell us what has already happened to us by faith:

> His divine power has granted to us all things that pertain to life and godliness, through the knowledge of him who called us by his own glory and virtue; by which he has granted to us his precious and exceedingly great promises; that through these you may become partakers of the divine nature, having escaped from the corruption that is in the world by lust.

Notice all the things God gave to us by faith that Peter describes in this passage. We have everything we need for life and godliness, we know God, and we have escaped the corruption that is in the world because of lust. Because of these wonderful promises, we can become partakers of his divine nature.

Peter then teaches us to "add to" our faith. You may have heard as often as I have that we cannot add to our faith. Peter had not heard that evangelical tradition. He commanded us to add to our faith. Because of all those things that we already have, as described in verses 3-4, we can supplement our faith with virtue, knowledge, self-control, perseverance, godliness, brotherly kindness, and love (vv. 5-7). If we do so, we will not be unfruitful in our faith (v.8), we will make our calling and election sure (v. 10), and we will be—future tense—richly supplied with an entrance into the everlasting kingdom of our Lord Jesus Christ (v. 11).

In Paul's letter to the Galatians, we see something similar. In the past tense, the Galatians began in the Spirit (3:3); in the present tense God is supplying the Spirit to them (3:4); and if they walk in the Spirit and avoid the works of the flesh, they will inherit the kingdom of God (5:19-21).

Paul even wrote a passage specifically distinguishing between the past and future parts of our salvation:

> Much more then, being now justified by his blood, we will be saved from God's wrath through him. For if, while we were enemies, we were reconciled to God through the death of his Son, much more, being reconciled, we will be saved by his life. (Rom. 5:9-10)

Notice the tenses in this passage. In the past tense, we are justified by his blood and reconciled by his death. In the future tense, we are saved from God's wrath through him and through his life. This is a reference to the fact that we live our life here on earth by faith in Christ and by the power of the Spirit. Paul described this in Galatians 2:20, where he wrote:

> I have been crucified with Christ, and it is no longer I that live, but Christ living in me. That life which I now live in the flesh, I live by faith in the Son of God, who loved me, and gave himself up for me.

His death and his blood have brought us—past tense—into justification and have reconciled us to God. We then live by his life and do the good works that God has created us in King Jesus to do (Eph. 2:10). In this way, his life will save us—future tense—from God's wrath.

All of this precludes boasting, even though our works will be judged. It is Jesus' life that saves us. We cannot boast when we do good works. We are simply making use of the exceptional greatness of his power (Eph. 1:19) and laying hold of the great and precious promises (2 Pet. 1:4) that God has supplied us with. As the Apostle Paul put it to the Corinthians, "What do you have that you didn't receive? But if you did receive it, why do you boast as if you had not received it?" (1 Cor. 4:7).

This pattern of salvation by faith in the past tense, the power of the Spirit in the present tense, and a judgment by works in our future is consistent in the writings of all the apostles except John. The Apostle John is a very interesting exception to this rule, and we must therefore give special attention to his writings.

The Writings of the Apostle John

Unlike all the other New Testament writers, John does not speak of salvation by faith in the past tense. In fact, he only uses the word "saved" three times in his Gospel. Each time, he simply tells us that Jesus is going to save the world (Jn. 3:17; 5:34; 10:9).

Nor does he speak of eternal life as a future reward at the judgment, as other New Testament writers do, but as a current possession of the believer. He does, however, in quoting Jesus, teach that the judgment will be based on works.

> Don't marvel at this, for the hour comes in which all who are in the tombs will hear his voice, and will come out; those who have done good, to the resurrection of life; and those who have done evil, to the resurrection of judgment. (Jn. 5:28-29)

John's Gospel is unique. It is so unique that we call the other three Gospels "the synoptic Gospels." "Synoptic" means "taking the same point of view." Obviously, this implies that the Gospel of John does not take the same point of view. The Bible Project tells us that while 90% of Mark is repeated in Matthew and Luke, 90% of John's Gospel is unique.[58]

This does not mean that we can interpret John in such a way that he contradicts the other New Testament writers. While John's perspective might be different, the apostles handed down one faith to the churches (Jude 1:3). The churches of the various apostles

---

[58] Strauss, 2020, "John: The Gospel of the Eternal Son Who Reveals the Father"

were in unity for centuries no matter which apostle founded them. Many early Christian writers testify to this. For example, in the late first century the church in Rome wrote a letter to the church in Corinth saying:

> The apostles have preached the Gospel to us from the Lord Jesus Christ. Jesus Christ [has done so] from God. Christ, therefore, was sent by God, and the apostles by Christ.[59]

Clement, who wrote this on behalf of the church in Rome, tells us there is one Gospel that came from the apostles, not differing Gospels from Paul, John, Peter, or others.

In the early second century, the bishop of Antioch, home church of the apostle Paul, encouraged the church in Magnesia[60] to "be established in the doctrines of the Lord and the apostles."[61] Again, they knew of only one set of doctrines from the apostles, not many.

Later in the second century and on into the third, prominent Christians would write defenses of the faith that leaned on the argument that all churches everywhere taught the same faith from the apostles. One wrote:

> The Church, having received this preaching and this faith, although scattered throughout the whole world, yet, as if occupying but one house, carefully preserves it. She also believes these points [of doctrine] just as if she had but one soul, and one and the same heart, and she proclaims them, and teaches them, and hands them down, with perfect harmony, as if she possessed only one mouth.[62]

If we pit John's words against Paul's, or against any of the other Gospel writers, we make the Bible to contradict itself. Because John's churches were in so much unity with the churches of other apostles that they seemed to have one heart and one mouth, we must not pit John against Paul or James. We must

---

[59] Clement, c. 81-96, "1 Clement," ch. 42
[60] Magnesia was twelve miles from Ephesus in what is now western Turkey.
[61] Ignatius, 107 or 116, "Epistle to the Magnesians," ch. 13
[62] Irenaeus, c. 185, *Against Heresies*, Bk. I, ch. 10, par. 2

search their words to see how they agree, not form doctrines based on our favorite apostle.

Living in the Now

One of the more obvious features of John's Gospel and letters is their focus on the present. The ones believing have eternal life, and the ones disbelieving do not have eternal life (e.g., Jn. 3:16, 36; 6:47). This cannot be mistaken for a faith that does not include love and good works, however. John is careful to say that only those who practice righteousness are righteous as Jesus is righteous (1 Jn. 3:7). Those who do not practice righteousness nor love their spiritual siblings are not of God. In fact, this lack of love and righteousness marks them as children of the devil (1 Jn. 3:10).

Though John is consistently quoted in defense of salvation by faith alone, his idea of faith may be the most stringent in the New Testament. Yes, he says he wrote 1 John to assure those who believe that they have eternal life (1 Jn. 5:13), but look at what he wrote in 1 John!

- "If we say we have fellowship with him and walk in the darkness, we lie, and don't tell the truth" (1:6).
- "One who says, 'I know him,' and doesn't keep his commandments, is a liar, and the truth is not in him" (2:4).
- "He who says he is in the light and hates his brother is in the darkness even until now" (2:9).
- "Don't love the world or the things that are in the world. If anyone loves the world, the Father's love isn't in him." (2:15).

1 John 5:13 teaches that we who believe in Jesus can know we have eternal life, but only if we walk in the light, keep his commandments, love our brothers and sisters, and do not love the world. Otherwise, in John's loving words, we are liars.

I could go on. That was just chapters 1 and 2. John is intently focused on the present. Those who are loving the saints, walking in the light, and turning away from worldly lusts have eternal life. Those who are not doing so do not know God.

This is not because John was condemning or judgmental. He is careful to quote Jesus as saying that he came into the world to save it rather than condemn it (Jn. 3:17). We who are believing will never come into condemnation (Jn. 5:24). Instead, John was supremely confident that when eternal life, the life of Jesus, entered a person they would be transformed. Those who are born of God, he wrote, are not in the habit of sinning (1 John 3:9).

1 John 3:9

First John 3:9 needs to be addressed here, so let's pause to do so. Many Bible versions, including the WEB, which I have been using, read something to the effect of "Whoever is born of God doesn't commit sin." It is important not to interpret this verse so that it contradicts the rest of 1 John. First John 1:7 to 2:2 tells us what to do when we sin, something John would not have written if he thought those born of God *never* sin. He even writes that the one who says he has no sin is deceiving himself (1:8).

The solution to the puzzling assertion of 1 John 3:9 is that the Greek verbs used by the New Testament writers communicate much more than our English verbs can.[63] Commentators point out several good interpretations of 1 John 3:9 that do not contradict earlier portions of the letter and do not include the impossible idea that born-again people never sin.[64]

Despite John's focus on the now, he did not neglect to warn us of the judgment by works. I quoted John 5:28-29 above. but in John 15, Jesus also tells us:

> If a man doesn't remain in me, he is thrown out as a branch and is withered; and they gather them, throw them into the fire, and they are burned. (Jn. 15:6)

As said, in John's eyes to be in Jesus is to be transformed. Thus, he writes, "He who remains in me, and I in him, bears much fruit, for apart from me you can do nothing" (Jn. 15:5). Our simple job is to remain in faith, continuing to trust in the power of God to transform us. Paul uses similar words, saying:

---

[63] Keating, n.d., "Greek Verb Tenses (Intermediate Discussion)"

[64] Bible Hub provides several commentaries for each verse of our Bibles on their website. The commentaries on 1 John 3:9 are at https://biblehub.com/commentaries/1_john/3-9.htm.

> You, being in past times alienated and enemies in your mind in your evil deeds, yet now he has reconciled in the body of his flesh through death, to present you holy and without defect and blameless before him, if it is so that you continue in the faith, grounded and steadfast, and not moved away from the hope of the Good News. (Col. 1:22-23)

With this thought in mind, Paul adds:

> As therefore you received Christ Jesus, the Lord, walk in him, rooted and built up in him, and established in the faith, even as you were taught, abounding in it in thanksgiving. (Col. 2:6)

This should be enough to establish that John and Paul taught the same way to love and live righteously and the same way to be rewarded with life at the judgment. We are to live by the life of Christ, never losing track of that focus, intently pursuing him. We need to "abound" in that life with "thanksgiving." As Paul wrote in Romans 5:9-10, "... we will be saved from God's wrath through him ... we will be saved by his life."

Despite this very similar reliance on the life of Christ in us, we must address the distinction in their use of "eternal" life.

John and Eternal Life

John is the only New Testament writer who calls the life that we have as followers of Jesus "eternal life." He is not the only New Testament writer who says we have received life as a reward for our faith in Jesus, but he is the only one who calls it "eternal life." Paul writes about the life of Jesus in us often. In Colossians 3, for example, he writes:

> For you died, and your life is hidden with Christ in God. When Christ, our life, is revealed, then you will also be revealed with him in glory. (Col. 1:3-4)

Colossians 3 is just one example. Paul uses the word "life" 49 times in his letters.[65] John and Paul agree that we have life from Jesus now, but Paul does not call it eternal life. We cannot know why for certain, but I would argue that it is because Paul knew we

---

[65] Fifty-two times if Hebrews was written by Paul

will not keep that life if we live in sin. We do not yet possess that life eternally. Instead, we will "die" if we live according to the flesh (Rom. 8:13; Gal. 6:7).

John, however, feels free to call the life we received from Jesus "eternal life" because the life is eternal whether we possess it eternally, possess it temporarily, or never possess it all. "Eternal" is the nature of the life itself. John writes:

> That which was from the beginning, that which we have heard, that which we have seen with our eyes, that which we saw, and our hands touched, concerning the Word of life (the life was revealed, and we have seen, and testify, and declare to you the life, the eternal life, which was with the Father, and was revealed to us). (1 Jn. 1:1-2; parentheses in original)

Just as John writes at the beginning of his Gospel that the Word of God came to earth in Jesus, so at the beginning of his first epistle he writes that the eternal life of God came to the earth in Jesus. In John's understanding, eternal life is the life of Jesus. When Jesus came to earth from heaven, the apostles saw and touched eternal life. John restates this in the fifth chapter saying:

> God gave to us eternal life, and this life is in his Son. He who has the Son has the life. He who doesn't have God's Son doesn't have the life. (5:11-12)

To John, eternal life is simply the life of Jesus. If God's Son is living in one of us, then eternal life is in us as well. If he is not living in us, then eternal life is not in us. It is not our possession of the life that is eternal, but the life itself is eternal.

What then, we must ask, is the life that John says will be given to those who have done good when he raises the dead? (Jn. 5:28-29). I would argue that this is the immortality spoken of in Romans 2:7. If we have believed in Jesus, walked in the light, kept Jesus' commandments, and loved the brothers and sisters, then we had eternal life throughout our time of believing. We had that life because we had the Son, and eternal life is in the Son. On the last day, when immortality is awarded at the judgment, then eternal life will be in us as well as in Jesus. We will become like Jesus, who has had eternal life from the beginning. We will become his brothers (Rom. 8:29) by adoption (Rom. 8:23), immortal sons of the immortal Father and immortal brothers of the Son.

I must pause to tell you that I do not consider that last paragraph as solid as the rest of this book. Perhaps there is a better way to understand the difference between Paul's use of eternal life and John's. On the other hand, both John and Paul tell us there will be a judgment, and the only ones who will receive life at that judgment are those who have "done good" (Jn. 5:28-29).

I am presenting this as an explanation for John's unique use of "eternal life." You may see things differently, and perhaps you will find a better explanation among trained scholars. My concern is rebuilding God's firm foundation, introducing you to the judgment by works, and encouraging you to live by the Spirit, use the Scriptures, and walk by grace so that you do good works and receive an abundant entrance into Jesus' everlasting kingdom. Explaining John's unique use of "eternal life" is not relevant to my purpose. It was enough to show you that John agrees with the other New Testament writers on the subjects covered in this book. It just seemed wrong to leave you with no explanation at all of John's unique use of "eternal life," even if that explanation was an uncertain one.

John agrees with everything I have written about the judgment and salvation. We are saved by believing that Jesus is the Christ, the Son of God (Jn. 20:31); we work out our salvation by walking by the Spirit so that we obey God (1 Jn. 2:3-4) and love one another (1 John 4:19). Having borne good fruit by abiding in Jesus (Jn. 15:1-8), we are rewarded with immortality (John 5:28-29). John is even clear to say that if we do not bear fruit, then even though we were attached to the vine as branches, we will be cut off and thrown in the fire (John 15:6).

In that sense, John is not unique. He had no place for a Christian life that does not include good works. 1 John 5:13 lets you "know that you have eternal life" because the rest of the letter shows that everyone who walks in the light, keeps Jesus' commandments, does righteousness, and loves has eternal life. As a result, he does offer assurance of eternal life to Christians, but only if we "assure our hearts before him" by loving in deed and truth rather than in word or tongue (1 Jn. 3:18-22).

We do not ever want to pit one apostle against another, nor even all the writers of the New Testament against John's unique Gospel and letters. I pray to God, and I trust that I have not compromised anything the apostle John said in this chapter. Of all the apostles, his warnings about the necessity of obedience and love are the strongest. Yes, he emphasized faith, but he defines faith just as it is defined in this book.

1. The faith that saves is faith that Jesus is the Christ, the Son of God (Jn. 20:31).
2. The faith that gives eternal life (1 Jn. 5:13-14) is a faith that walks in the light (1 Jn. 1:6-7), keeps Jesus' commandments (1 Jn. 2:3-4), does not love the things of the world (1 Jn. 2:15-16), practices righteousness (1 Jn. 3:7-10), and loves the saints (1 Jn. 4:7-8).
3. The faith that saves requires us to persevere to the end. Branches that do not "remain" in Jesus—which means that they were once in him—will be cut off and burned because they do not bear fruit (Jn. 15:2, 6).

We see, then, that John teaches the same truths that we have seen throughout this book with a greater emphasis on how things are in the present than how they will be in the future.

1 John 2:19: "They Were Never of Us"

Thirty-four years and six months ago, I was invited to a Bible study by a lovely Baptist girl who had no idea what she was getting herself into, nor what she was getting me and the members of the Bible study into.

The Bible study was on Romans 11. There were fourteen of us sitting around a long table. It began with the leader, who was sitting at the far end of the table from me, asking the person on her left to read verses 1-3.

I knew Romans 11, and I knew that it had a passage that would not be popular in a Baptist Bible study, especially if I was the one commenting on it. Rather than listen to the young man reading verses 1-3, I quickly counted the number of people between him and me. I realized I was going to be asked to read and comment on that controversial passage. I panicked a bit.

When I visited the Baptist church, I had promised God that I would not cause trouble. I would avoid doctrinal conflicts. I was trying to learn how to live in unity in the midst of many divided denominations. The kind of doctrinal conflict I could expect when the Bible study leader asked me to read those verses was exactly the kind I had promised God I would avoid.

If you already know which verses I was asked to read, congratulations on knowing your Bible so well. If not, here they are:

> You will say then, "Branches were broken off, that I might be grafted in." True; by their unbelief they were broken off, and you stand by your faith. Don't be conceited, but fear; for if God didn't spare the natural branches, neither will he spare you. See then the goodness and severity of God. Toward those who fell, severity; but toward you, goodness, if you continue in his goodness; otherwise you also will be cut off. (Rom. 11:19-22)

I had already been trying to figure out a way to do justice to the passage without bringing up the controversial topic of eternal security. Keep in mind, I was not 60 years old, as I am now. I was young and relatively shy. Also, I did not want to be a party to increasing the division in the church. I wanted to avoid controversy.

The leader erased all the comments I was preparing in my mind. She did not ask, "What do you think these verses mean?" She asked, "Do you think this means you can lose your salvation?"

I literally dropped my head on the table. I prayed, "God, this isn't my fault. I did not choose this battle."

Then I raised my head up and said, "Yes. Yes, I do."

That was the end of the planned Bible study. It transformed to an argument instantaneously. Romans 11:19-22 was not brought up for the rest of the night. Instead, the night went like this:

THEM: How can a person lose eternal life?

ME: It is the life that is eternal, not your possession of it.

THEM: How can a born-again person be unborn?

ME: They can't, but they can die.

THEM: The Bible says we can't be snatched out of Jesus hand.

ME: You're right, but you can walk away.

Then:

ME: Listen, it appears I have had these debates a lot more than you have. I have heard all these arguments many times before, and I have answers for them. You should ask me about 1 John 2:19. I have no answer for that verse.

Oddly enough, not one of the other thirteen people present looked up 1 John 2:19 at my request. The pretty Baptist girl who invited me, who is now my wife, tells me that they did not want to look ignorant and have to look it up. Instead, they kept throwing out arguments I had heard many times before. I told them at least three times that I could not answer 1 John 2:19, and at least three times, they just ignored me.

First John 2:19 reads:

> They went out from us, but they did not belong to us; for if they had belonged to us, they would have remained with us. However, they went out so that it might be made clear that none of them belongs to us.

It sure seemed to me, at the time, that this verse says that if a Christian falls away, or leaves the church, it is proof they were never saved. They did not lose their salvation; they never had it.

Even to this day, that seems the plainest way to interpret the passage. It is true that, in context, "they" that went out from us, are the "many antichrists" that have come already (1 Jn. 2:18). It is possible that John is not talking about Christians in general at all. He may be speaking only of those teachers that have been teaching the falsehoods that prompted John's letter.

Scholars agree upon that John's letter is addressing a sect of the gnostics known as "docetists."[66] Docetists denied that anything "material," which included everything that can be seen, can be good. Thus, they taught that the Christ could not have come to earth in human flesh, but only in spirit. First John 4:2-3 rejects this teaching directly.

---

[66] e.g., Encyclopedia Britannica, Editors of, n.d., "Docetism"

A person teaching that Jesus Christ was a phantom or that an invisible Christ spirit rested on the physical Jesus, could easily be distinguished from Christians that had professed since baptism that Jesus was the Christ, had been born of a virgin, suffered physically on the cross, and rose from the dead bodily. Thus, it is plausible that John was speaking only of docetists when he said their leaving proves they were never of us.

While the above is a plausible, and perhaps even the best, interpretation of 1 John 2:19, it is not satisfying to me. If I am not satisfied, I am certainly not going to ask you to be satisfied.

There is also the possibility that John's emphasis on what is happening right now, in the present, explains 1 John 2:19. We have already discussed this emphasis of John's. Perhaps those who fall away establish themselves as always having fallen away, at least in John's eyes.

The parable of the ten virgins backs up this interpretation. In the parable, all the virgins are waiting for the bridegroom, and all of them have oil, which is generally interpreted as typifying the Holy Spirit. Five virgins run out of oil and must run out to buy more. The bridegroom, representing Christ, arrives while they are gone, and shuts the door. When the five foolish virgins return, the bridegroom refuses to open the door because he does not know them (Matt. 25:1-13).

Even though the five foolish virgins were once in, now that they are out, they not only cannot get back in, but they are unknown to the bridegroom. This does sound a lot like 1 John 2:19, and it also sounds like the doctrine that if a person falls away, they were never saved.

If this is nothing but perspective, it would not matter. For example, the writer of Hebrews contrasts those who live by faith with those who "shrink back to destruction" (Heb. 10:36-39). He speaks from Paul's perspective (and may even be Paul[67]), saying that those with faith can still shrink back and be destroyed. If 1 John 2:19 is about Christians in general, then John would say of

---

[67] Despite the fact that the King James Version titles Hebrews "Paul's Epistle to the Hebrews," no one knows who wrote it. Its authorship is hotly debated.

those same persons that they were never saved, but he would agree with the writer of Hebrews that they will be destroyed. If they both say those who shrink back will be destroyed, but the writer of Hebrews says they lost something, and John says they never had anything to lose. There is no difference in practical results. They are not living for Jesus, and destruction is their future either way. Whether they were saved in the past might be interesting, but it is not significant.

For me, and I am sure for most of those reading the book, concluding that John and the other New Testament writers are speaking from two different perspectives is not a very pleasant thought. Thus, I prefer the argument that John was only speaking of docetist teachers, whom he described as antichrists, in 1 John 2:19.

Additionally, in the twenty-first century, when I am writing this, the difference is not just perspective. There is a very significant practical difference between those who believe and teach eternal security and those who do not.

The evangelism training programs *Evangelism Explosion* and *Continuing Witness Training*, discussed in chapters one and two, teach their fledgling evangelists to immediately assure their converts that they have eternal life and can never lose it. Both programs teach the trainee evangelist to show the new convert John 6:47, which reads, "Most certainly, I tell you, he that believes in me has eternal life." The evangelist then assures them that they have eternal life on the basis of faith and faith only, which excludes the possibility of their doing anything to lose that eternal life.[68]

If you have ever been part of a church's evangelism program, then you know that once a person prays a prayer of salvation in their home, there is a good chance you will never see them again. Others will show up for church a few times, then disappear. Within two or three years the majority of those who prayed the prayer and were assured of eternal life will have discontinued all pretense of Christianity.

---

[68] Evangelism Explosion International, 2015, "Assurance"

Even Christians who hold to the doctrine of eternal security know this is true. It is impossible to participate in American evangelical Christianity for very long and deny that most people who pray a sinner's prayer do not follow through on their commitment.

It used to be that eternal-security churches taught that these "converts" who did not follow through were going to be saved anyway because works have nothing to do with salvation. This idea, that someone can be a Christian without at least trying to live like one, is absurd. When absurd ideas are exposed to the general public, as most ideas are in the information age, they are typically driven to the fringes of society. An eternal security that offers salvation to people who have made no effort to live like a Christian has been likewise banished to the fringes of Christianity because there is just no way to fit that idea into James 2:14-26, no matter how hard you try to twist the passage.

Today, eternal-security churches usually teach that a person who is saved, though he or she is not *required* to do good works, will do them as a natural result, or fruit of being saved. If they do not do good works, they say, it is because that person was never saved.

The problem remains, though, that those who believe in eternal security assure all converts, on the day that they pray a prayer of salvation, that they have eternal life and cannot lose it. Later, though, they will say, about the very same person, that they were never saved.

This is a great evil. You can quote 1 John 2:19 all you want, and it will still be evil to tell young Christians that they have eternal life and cannot lose it then, when they fall away, say they never had it.

Far better is to tell them what the apostles told them:
- Peter: "Be more diligent to make your calling and election sure. For if you do these things you will never stumble." (2 Pet. 1:10)
- Paul: "... he has reconciled in the body of his flesh through death, to present you holy and without defect

and blameless before him, if it is so that you continue in the faith, grounded and steadfast." (Col. 1:22-23)
- John: "My little children, let's not love in word only, or with the tongue only, but in deed and truth. And by this we know that we are of the truth, and persuade our hearts before him." (1 Jn. 3:18-19)

1 Corinthians 3:15: Saved, But As Through Fire

1 Corinthians 3:1-15 has not come up as we have researched "God's Firm Foundation." This is because it is not a foundational passage, but a more advanced teaching. As Hebrews 6:1 teaches, there is a time to leave behind "the teaching of the first principles of Christ." Nonetheless, one verse in 1 Corinthians 3 can be read to contradict everything we have seen in this book.

1 Corinthians 3:15 reads:

> If any man's work is burned, he will suffer loss, but he himself will be saved, but as through fire.

This verse, read by itself, sounds like the perfect proof text for eternal security, the teaching that a Christian will be saved even if he grows weary of doing good. Even if a man's work is all "wood, hay, or stubble" (1 Cor. 3:12), he will be saved. Only his work will burn up; the person will be saved.

The context of this verse, though, is decisive.

Typically, when someone references this verse, they tell me that even if their "works" are entirely wood, hay, and stubble, they will be saved. Notice, though, that "works" is never found in 1 Corinthians 3:1-15. "Work" is always singular.

Paul spends verses 1 through 7 talking about apostles who have taught in the Corinthian church. In verse 8, he writes, "He who plants and he who waters are the same, but each will receive his own reward according to his own labors."

He then describes these labors by saying:

> According to the grace of God which was given to me, as a wise master builder I laid a foundation, and another builds on it. But let each man be careful how he builds on it. For no one can lay any other foundation than that which has been laid,

> which is Jesus Christ. But if anyone builds on the foundation with gold, silver, costly stones, wood, hay, or stubble, each man's work will be revealed. For the Day will declare it, because it is revealed in fire; and the fire itself will test what sort of work each man's work is. (vv. 10-13)

Paul is not writing about good works; he is writing about the work of ministry, of service to the Corinthians. Paul laid a foundation in Corinth, just as I have laid a foundation in this book. The only foundation that can be laid is Jesus Christ. Now, if someone comes along and *by teaching, good or bad*, builds on that foundation—whether the apostle Paul's or mine—"the Day" will reveal whether that teaching was good or bad.

Despite the fact that teachers receive a stricter judgment (James 3:1), no teacher's salvation is on the line for incompetent teaching. God condemns those who complacently give in to the flesh (Gal. 6:7-9), not those who are incompetent. A teacher's works, good or bad, will determine their eternal destiny, not their "work," their teaching, no matter how skilled or unskilled it may be.

We find the opposite idea in Matthew 7:22-23, that skilled ministry will not save you if you live an unholy life. There we see people who served Jesus by prophesying, casting out demons, and working miracles, but who practiced iniquity. Despite all their service, Jesus turns them away as people he does not know because they did not live righteously.

Do Not Be Deceived

This chapter has addressed objections to God's Firm Foundation as described in this book. Objections can be good, as they force teachers to look at what they teach from the perspective of others. Objections can also be bad if they stop us from looking at important things. No matter what tradition you are from, and no matter how you have reacted to this book, there are some teachings of Scripture that you must not object to.

Those teachings begin with or include the words "Do not be deceived," and I will list those in the next chapter.

9. The "Do Not Be Deceived" Passages

There are several passages warning us, in explicit terms, against thinking we will receive eternal life without works. Obviously, those who believe we receive eternal life purely by faith try to avoid these verses. I want to put them where they belong, front and center:

I will just list the verses. They speak for themselves, but I am going to highlight the warnings anyway.

> **Don't be deceived.** God is not mocked, for whatever a man sows, that he will also reap. For he who sows to his own flesh will from the flesh reap corruption. But he who sows to the Spirit will from the Spirit reap eternal life. Let's not be weary in doing good, for we will reap in due season, if we don't give up. (Gal. 6:7-9)

> But sexual immorality, and all uncleanness or covetousness, let it not even be mentioned among you, as becomes saints; nor filthiness, nor foolish talking, nor jesting, which are not appropriate, but rather giving of thanks. **Know this for sure**, that no sexually immoral person, nor unclean person, nor covetous man, who is an idolater, has any inheritance in the Kingdom of Christ and God. **Let no one deceive you with empty words.** For because of these things, the wrath of God comes on the children of disobedience. Therefore don't be partakers with them. (Eph. 5:3-7)

> Beloved, while I was very eager to write to you about our common salvation, I was constrained to write to you exhorting you to **contend earnestly for the faith which was once for all delivered to the saints.** For there are certain men who crept in secretly, even those who were long ago written about for this condemnation: ungodly men, turning the grace of our God into indecency, and denying our only Master, God, and Lord, Jesus Christ. Now **I desire to remind you, though you already know this,** that the Lord, having saved a people out of the land of Egypt, afterward destroyed those who didn't believe. (Jude 1:3-5)

> Or **don't you know** that the unrighteous will not inherit God's Kingdom? **Don't be deceived**. Neither the sexually immoral, nor idolaters, nor adulterers, nor male prostitutes, nor homosexuals, nor thieves, nor covetous, nor drunkards, nor slanderers, nor extortionists, will inherit God's Kingdom. Some of you were such, but you were washed. But you were sanctified. But you were justified in the name of the Lord Jesus, and in the Spirit of our God. (1 Cor. 6:9-11)

In this final passage, from 1 John, we cannot forget John's love for the Greek present tense, which indicates continuous or progressive action.[69] John is not teaching that those born of God never commit a single sin, but that their life is marked by obedience, not by sin.

> Little children, **let no one lead you astray**. He who does righteousness is righteous, even as he is righteous. He who sins is of the devil, for the devil has been sinning from the beginning. To this end the Son of God was revealed: that he might destroy the works of the devil. Whoever is born of God doesn't commit sin, because his seed remains in him, and he can't sin, because he is born of God. In this the children of God are revealed, and the children of the devil. Whoever doesn't do righteousness is not of God, neither is he who doesn't love his brother. (1 Jn. 3:7-10)

Yes, many Christians disagree with the things written in this book. According to Scripture, they have been deceived, and we are warned not to be deceived along with them.

How could this have happened? How could so many people be deceived?

Perhaps Mark Twain explained best:

> ... a country's laws are written upon paper, and ... its customs are engraved upon brass. One may play with the one, but not with the other. It is less risky for a stranger to dance upon our Constitution in the public square than to affront one of our

---

[69] Keating, n.d., "Greek Verb Tenses (Intermediate Discussion)"

solidified customs. The one is merely eminently respectable, the other is sacred.[70]

What is true of countries and their laws has, over the centuries, proven just as true of churches and the Scriptures. It is less risk to twist, deny, convolute, and ignore the Bible than to affront the traditions of the Reformation.

I pray that I have uprooted these traditions and upheld Scripture gently, carefully, and slowly enough to convince you. If I have, it is very important I discuss with you how to implement these truths in the twenty-first century.

---

[70] Twain, 1906, letter to Charlotte Teller

10. Living Out God's Firm Foundation Today

Be Delivered from Disputing!

As I write this, the world is fighting a pandemic, COVID-19. There is another pandemic, however, that is going unchallenged:

> If anyone teaches a different doctrine and does not come forward with healthy words, those of our Lord Jesus Christ, and in the according-to-piety instruction, he is dulled, having knowledge of nothing, but diseased concerning inquiries and arguings over words, of which becomes envy, strife, blasphemies, bad opinions ... (1 Tim. 6:3-4, Apostolic Bible Polyglot[71])

You have probably never seen this translation of 1 Timothy 6:4. If you read through the verse, rather than skimming it as many readers do, the word "diseased" probably stood out to you. The Greek word is *noseo*, and its basic meaning is "sick." Thayer's Greek English Lexicon of the New Testament gives an additional meaning: "to be taken with such an interest in a thing as amounts to a disease, to have a morbid fondness for."[72] As my thirty-eight years of discussions with Christians prove, and as Facebook and every other social media outlet prove, a diseased obsession for "inquiries and arguings over words" is a thriving pandemic in our midst.

I beg of you not to use my book to spread this disease. If you need to wear a mask over your mouth like you do for COVID-19 to prevent infection, please do. For this disease, duct tape works even better than a medical mask. (If you use duct tape, be very careful not to cover your nose.)

I learned the phrase "obedience-based Bible interpretation" from Curtis Sergeant. In 2019, I attended one of his MetaCamps, as he calls them, near Birmingham, Alabama.[73] There I learned of discipleship movements that have reached more than 50 million people. The people in these movements are forming discipleship groups of 6 to 12 people that he calls "simple churches." I do not

---

[71] Apostolic Bible Polyglot, n.d., "1 Timothy 6:3-4"
[72] StudyBible.info, n.d., "G3352 νοσέω – Strong's Greek Lexicon Number"
[73] See metacamp.org (MetaCamp, 2020, "MetaCamp").

have time to explain how these simple churches connect in larger groups that include the biblical concepts of apostles, prophets, evangelists, shepherds, and teachers. You can look him up online and find out for yourself. Suffice it to say that his discipleship methods are extremely effective.

When I went to the MetaCamp, I found out that I disagree with Curtis on what the Bible teaches about evangelism. In a very respectable manner, as a learner and not a teacher, I questioned him on the subject, giving my reasons for asking. His answer did not persuade me. I also disagree with his method for presenting the Gospel. I think the way I present the Gospel is more like the apostles' Gospel than his is. Nonetheless ...

Jesus said that we would know true prophets by their fruit (Matt. 7:16,20). I apply this to true teachers as well. "A good tree can't produce evil fruit," said Jesus, "neither can a corrupt tree produce good fruit" (Matt. 7:18). Curtis Sergeant has excellent fruit. His fruit production is so great that I can hardly conceive of the number of people his disciples have trained.

I will never, for any reason, get in the way of men like that. People who produce good fruit are good teachers. In fact, Christian workers with mediocre theology and good fruit are proof positive that God does not care about the "arguings over words" that we are "morbidly obsessed with."

So why am I willing write a book disputing common American theology?

The teachings that matter are the ones that you can do (James 1:22). "All those who do his work have a good understanding" (Ps. 111:10). This is "obedience-based" Bible interpretation.

We are commanded to fight for sound (i.e., healthy) doctrine (2 Tim. 4:2-3), but very few of us know what healthy doctrine is. The very last letters Paul wrote were those to Timothy and Titus. In 2 Timothy 4:7, he wrote, "I have fought the good fight. I have finished the course." These letters were the last teachings Paul left behind. In them he was careful to explain healthy teaching:

> Say **the things which fit sound doctrine**, that older men should be temperate, sensible, sober minded, sound in faith, in love, and in perseverance: and that older women likewise be

> reverent in behavior, not slanderers nor enslaved to much wine, teachers of that which is good, that they may train the young wives to love their husbands, to love their children, to be sober minded, chaste, workers at home, kind, being in subjection to their own husbands, that God's word may not be blasphemed. Likewise, exhort the younger men to be sober minded. In all things show yourself an example of good works. In your teaching, show integrity, seriousness, incorruptibility, and soundness of speech that can't be condemned, that he who opposes you may be ashamed, having no evil thing to say about us. (Tit. 2:1-7)

It turns out that healthy doctrine is focused on all the same things that Scripture, the new birth, grace, the fellowship of the church, and the atonement are focused on! Sound doctrine is to be "temperate, sensible, sober-minded, sound in faith, in love, and in perseverance."

The next time sound doctrine is brought up to you, tell the person that you are consumed with being sound in faith, love, and perseverance. When the other person asks why that came up, read them Titus 2:1-2. It might be fun to follow up with 1 Timothy 1:3-6:

> Command certain men not to teach a different doctrine, and not to pay attention to myths and endless genealogies, which cause disputes, rather than God's stewardship, which is in faith—**but the goal of this command is love**, out of a pure heart and a good conscience and sincere faith, **from which things some, having missed the mark, have turned away to vain talking**.

The words "sound doctrine" are only found in the letters to Timothy and Titus (1 Tim. 1:10; 2 Tim. 4:3; Tit. 1:9; 2:1). For those of you with a morbid fondness for disputing, I urge you to read the context of those verses. In fact, just read all three letters. Hopefully, that is the medicine you need. You must take the medicine regularly, though. Many of you will need extremely high doses.

The alternative is learning the way I did, by being diseased enough to butt heads with other diseased minds until I was dazed and could not take it anymore. An early third-century apologist once wrote, "A controversy over the Scriptures can, clearly, produce no other effect than to help to upset either the stomach or the brain."[74] That advice is 1,800 years old! I read that advice in 1990, and I still upset my stomach and brain for another five years! Please learn from Tertullian's advice and my foolishness!

That said, one of my calls to action is to attend a Curtis Sergeant MetaCamp. We may not see eye-to-eye on what the Scriptures say about evangelism, but he thoroughly prepares and equips those he sends. Further, he has more fruit than me. This excites me. It is Jesus who must be glorified, not us. I am not jealous of his fruit. I do not have the same calling he does; I have my own fruit based on my own calling. His fruit is mounted up much higher than mine, so my wife and I are giving ourselves to implementing his training in our own life and ministry.

Other Calls to Action

My other calls to action, besides being saved from the "morbid obsession with disputation" epidemic, arise naturally out of what I have taught here:

- Believe in your heart that God raised Jesus from the dead and confess with your mouth that Jesus is Lord (Rom. 10:9-10). Then be baptized for the *aphesis* of sins and receive the Holy Spirit (Acts 2:38; 22:16).
- Consider yourself dead to sin and alive to God in Jesus Christ (Rom. 6:11).
- Read the Scriptures and use them to teach, reprove, correct, and instruct in righteousness (2 Tim. 3:16-17). Find people who will do the same for you. This is church life. Do this in and out of the assembly (Heb. 3:13; 10:24-25).
- Deny ungodliness and worldly lusts, and live soberly, righteously, and godly. Grace teaches us to do so (Tit. 2:11-12), and walking by the Spirit makes it possible (Rom. 8:3-13; Gal. 5:16-25).
- Assemble with other disciples, at least one or two, and get to know each other enough that you can provoke to love and good works and exhort one another (Heb. 10:24-25). Again,

---

[74] Tertullian, c. 197-220, "The Prescription Against Heretics," ch. 16

see 1 Thessalonians 5:14 for what I believe is the best working definition of exhortation.

I will explain some of these more fully.

Consider Yourself Dead to Sin (Rom. 6:11)

It is amazing the role that your mind plays in being a disciple. Paul tells us to "be transformed by the renewing of your mind" (Rom. 12:2). When he wanted to bring change to the church of Corinth, Paul said he would do it with spiritual weapons that would:

> ... throw down ... strongholds, throw down imaginations and every high thing that is exalted against the knowledge of God and bring every thought into captivity to the obedience of Christ. (2 Cor. 10:4-5)

It is a mind set on the Spirit that is life and peace (Rom. 8:5-6). It as we "see" the glory of the Lord as in a mirror that we are transformed into that image (2 Cor. 3:18). When it is hard to go forward, we are to "look to" Jesus and "consider him" (Heb. 12:2-3).

The way we think of ourselves is critical. Often, Christians say of themselves that they are "sinners saved by grace." If we mean we *were* sinners, but now we are saved by grace, then this saying is good. If we mean we are still sinners, then we are not saved by grace. The one who practices sin is not born of God; in fact, he or she is a child of the devil (1 Jn. 3:7-10). We *were* sinners, but now that we are under grace, sin does not have power over us (Rom. 6:14). Instead, we have been redeemed from all iniquity, and grace is teaching us to deny ungodliness and worldly lusts and to live soberly, godly, and righteously (Tit. 2:11-14).

Walk in the Light

> "He who does the truth comes to the light that his works may be revealed, that they have been done in God." (John 3:21)

Those who walk in darkness, who hide from God, will be condemned (John 3:19). Jesus brought light to mankind (Jn. 1:4-5), so it makes no sense to call yourself his follower and live in darkness. Exposing your deeds, good or bad, to God so that he may cleanse you (1 Jn. 1:7) and to your brothers and sisters in Christ so they may pray for you (James 5:16).

The Church

It is heartbreaking to me that it is so hard to find a church that is not only family, but a family of disciples. Jesus said that we cannot be his disciples unless we take up our cross daily, deny ourselves, and follow him (Luke 9:23). More pointedly, he said that we cannot be his disciples unless we forsake our possessions (Luke 14:26-33).

Jesus was not talking about walking around naked and homeless any more than he was talking about carrying a big piece of wood around. Jesus' concern was for other people. The apostles and their churches responded to Jesus' teaching by loving and sharing. Yes, the first church in Jerusalem had such need that disciples were selling their lands and possessions to help create that first community (Acts 2:43-45). Later, though, as the church spread, this giving and sharing was only as needed (cf. 2 Corinthians 8-9).

Know, though, that the sharing going on in the churches was as much for the givers as the recipients. Yes, there were rich saints in the churches, but Paul warned them:

> Charge those who are rich in this present world that they not be arrogant, nor have their hope set on the uncertainty of riches, but on the living God, who richly provides us with everything to enjoy; that they do good, that they be rich in good works, that they be ready to distribute, willing to share; laying up in store for themselves a good foundation against the time to come, that they may lay hold of eternal life. (1 Tim. 6:17-19)

Just before that charge, he wrote:

> For we brought nothing into the world, and we certainly can't carry anything out. But having food and clothing, we will be content with that. But those who are determined to be rich fall into a temptation, a snare, and many foolish and harmful lusts, such as drown men in ruin and destruction. For the love of

money is a root of all kinds of evil. Some have been led astray from the faith in their greed, and have pierced themselves through with many sorrows. (1 Tim. 6:7-10)

This kind of thinking is more forgotten, at least in the United States, than even the foundational teachings found in this book. As Jesus said, if you want to build on the rock, you need to hear and obey his teachings (Matt. 7:24-27). One of his teachings was that it was difficult for a rich man to enter the kingdom of heaven (Matt. 19:23-24). This is because treasure on earth captures the heart. Jesus did not say, "For where your heart is, there will your treasure be," but "For where your treasure is, there will your heart be also" (Matt. 6:21). Treasure will draw your heart whether you try to focus your heart elsewhere or not. Doing good, being rich in good works, being ready to distribute, and being willing to share (1 Tim. 6:18) was Paul's prescription for the temptation and snare that comes with wealth (1 Tim. 6:9).

Even more lost is the idea that our assemblies need to include knowing one another well enough to provoke to love and good works (Heb. 10:24-25). Yes, that needs to go on outside the assemblies as well (Heb. 3:13; 1 Thess. 5:14), but Hebrews 10:24-25 is talking about in the assemblies. Most churches do not do Bible studies on 1 Corinthians 14, and most pastors do not preach sermons on it. Nonetheless, 1 Corinthians 14 is the only direction given to the churches regarding how they should meet!

In this horrific modern situation, you must find other disciples to meet within smaller groups. If you can find disciples willing to exhort one another day by day in your traditional church, that is the best thing of all. I have nothing against corporate singing and long sermons. I listen to sermons online occasionally and recommend you do so as well. I have occasionally given long teachings myself in the community I am part of. I am not suggesting you leave whatever Sunday morning meeting you attend; I am exhorting you to obey biblical guidelines for meetings *in addition* to any tradition-based services you may wish to attend.

Finding a Church

Many of you, especially readers of this book, have had trouble fitting into any modern church model. I have two kinds of advice for you. I have advice for finding Christians with whom you can fellowship, but I also have advice to help prevent you from being destroyed by your own theology and your confidence in it.

It is time, I think, to address the other sentence inscribed on God's firm foundation: "The Lord knows those who are his" (2 Tim. 2:19).

It is possible to consider yourself a better judge of who is your brother and sister than God is. It is common among those frustrated with traditional Christianity and traditional Christians to cut off everyone, even those that are trying to follow Jesus and have the Spirit of God. We cut them off because they are not "like-minded" or because they do not meet our standards.

God says, though:

> Who are you who judge another's servant? To his own lord he stands or falls. Yes, he will be made to stand, for God has power to make him stand. (Rom. 14:4)

I am not denying that churches should put out the wicked from among them (1 Cor. 5:13). Instead, I am saying that judging with humility is commanded by our Lord and by his apostles. "The Lord knows those who are his" is Paul's way of saying, "You probably *do not* know who are his."

Again, I am not denying that churches should put out the wicked from among them (1 Cor. 5:13). I encourage Christians to follow Jesus' command to go to a brother or sister who has offended you by yourself, then with another brother or two (or sister or two), and then present them to the church. I also encourage you to think about, understand, believe, and obey Jesus' parable regarding the wheat and the tares.

> [Jesus] set another parable before them, saying, "The Kingdom of Heaven is like a man who sowed good seed in his field, but while people slept, his enemy came and sowed darnel weeds also among the wheat, and went away. But when the blade sprang up and produced grain, then the darnel weeds appeared also. The servants of the householder came and said to him, 'Sir, didn't you sow good seed in your field? Where did these darnel weeds come from?'

"He said to them, 'An enemy has done this.'

"The servants asked him, 'Do you want us to go and gather them up?'

"But he said, 'No, lest perhaps while you gather up the darnel weeds, you root up the wheat with them. Let both grow together until the harvest, and in the harvest time I will tell the reapers, "First, gather up the darnel weeds, and bind them in bundles to burn them; but gather the wheat into my barn."'" (Matt. 13:24-30)

There are important things to notice in this parable. Who sowed the darnel [the "tares" in other translations]? Who are the servants, and what were they to do with the darnel weeds? Who is it that will remove the darnel weeds and when?

Yes, the devil sowed the darnel weeds [or "tares"]. Tares are children of the devil, and they will not be saved on the last day. Nonetheless, we are not to remove them. Jesus will remove the weeds on the last day.

Again, I am not talking about the wicked. It can be hard to distinguish between darnel weeds and wheat until harvest-time comes, and the wheat sprout heads. There are other plants that do not look like wheat. Those are the wicked (1 Cor. 5:13), the divisive (Tit. 3:10), and the openly unbelieving (2 Cor. 6:14-16). Those should be separated and evangelized, not made part of the church. But the tares? The darnel weeds that look like Christians should be allowed to grow among the wheat until the day Jesus does the reaping.

There is only one way to unity. According to Scripture, we must diligently preserve the unity of the Spirit (Eph. 4:3). We do not *create* the unity of the Spirit; we preserve it. If we will do this, and if we will learn how to build up the church and serve, speaking the truth in love to one another, each part doing its share, then we will grow together in love (Eph. 4:12-16). The result will be unity of the faith (Eph. 4:13).

This is true whether you love your Sunday morning church meeting or whether you never set foot in a traditional church service again.

You must believe that unity comes from the Spirit of God. I cannot help you find like-minded people. I can only help you find like-spirited people. The Holy Spirit knows the Holy Spirit, and he will put you with other Spirit-filled people *if you will not harm them*.

Teaching true scriptural principles that divide Christian from Christian harms people. It is true that a lot of people who claim to be Christian have simply joined the Christian religion. They do not have the Spirit of God, and you can never unite with them. Nonetheless, you are commanded to maintain the unity the Holy Spirit established (Eph. 4:3), not one you established, even his unity steps on, or even tromps all over, your interpretation of Scripture.

I am convinced that most of my long searching for real church life was to change me.

I believe God has been calling and preparing me to write this book for almost 40 years. The division I encountered early in my Christian life, my distaste for it, and my passioned resolve to find out just what the apostles taught to their churches were all put in my life to prepare me for writing this book, this set of teachings.

I have a powerful argument for the accuracy of these teachings. I found them on my own, in the Scriptures, by fiercely warring against my own biases and preconceptions. Along, the way I fought just as fiercely against the embarrassment and anger I felt when someone found error in what I taught. I lived what I taught, that you will never lose and argument if you give up and switch to the winning side.

As a result, when I was introduced to the early church fathers in 1990 by David Bercot's book, *Will the Real Heretics Please Stand Up*,[75] I already agreed with them on almost every subject Bercot covered.

To rediscover the teachings of the church fathers on my own, purely from the Scriptures, without influence from the fathers themselves nor anyone who had read them, is powerful evidence

---

[75] 1989, Scroll Publishing

that what I found in the Scriptures was accurate. When I first realized this, I made it my ambition to teach what I had found.

Unity, however, does not come from brilliant discoveries but from the Spirit of God. No matter how true my discoveries were, my theology was a danger to those around me because of my pride and my "diseased" obsession with arguing over words (1 Tim. 6:3-4, Apostolic Bible Polyglot[76]).

It took me a long time to be cured of this disease, especially because those who agreed with me were quick to pat me on the back, but I have been healing for 25 years. I believe I am currently in remission from that awful cancer.

Today, I have two dear friends who are pastors of traditional churches. Neither would appreciate me referring to them as traditional and, in practice, they are leaving much tradition behind because they are obedient to God's Spirit. Both were shocked, and displeased, to find out that I believe Christians will be judged as recorded in Romans 2:5-8. They cannot even consider the idea that we must do good works to be rewarded with eternal life. They love Jesus, they would do anything for him, and they are godly, Spirit-filled, and bear good fruit. Through much of my Christian life I would have ignored them. I would have failed to diligently maintain the unity of the Spirit in the bond of peace. I would have cared more about correcting their theology than preserving the unity God himself gave us.

Jesus prayed for this unity, a unity so great that it is like the fellowship of the Father and Son themselves!! (Jn. 17:20-23). It is impossible to overestimate such a gift but, in our ignorance, we throw it away at the slightest inconvenience or offense.

Dividing people bound together by the Spirit of God is foundational error, a foundational sin. "The Lord knows those are his" is inscribed on God's firm foundation. Those who divide the church are servants of their own belly (Rom. 16:17-18) and are to be rejected (Tit. 3:10).

At one time, that was me.

---

[76] Apostolic Bible Polyglot, n.d., "1 Timothy 6:3-4"

I am not wise enough to guide you to those that our Lord wants you to be joined in Spirit with. I can give you principles founded on the Bible. One of those principles is that the Bible is not the "sole" rule for faith and practice. (Perhaps it is better to say that our interpretation of the Bible is not the sole rule for faith and practice.) Instead, "those who are led by the Spirit of God, these are children of God" (Rom. 8:14). Or, as Jesus said:

> "You search the Scriptures, because you think that in them you have eternal life; and these are they which testify about me. Yet you will not come to me, that you may have life." (Jn. 5:39-40)

The best advice I can give you is to go to Jesus and go to Jesus and go to Jesus. Let the Spirit guide you to others with the Spirit. Diligently maintain your unity with them in the bond of peace. Help each other to grow closer and closer to Jesus and be better and better followers of the Spirit of God. Get to know one another well enough that you can provoke one another to love and good works by speaking the truth in love and humility. Remember, healthy doctrine has much more to do with obedience to Jesus than it does to things we can only speculate about (Tit. 2:1-15).

Disciple-Making Movements

Finally, one of the greatest movements of all time is taking place all over the world, both in free countries and countries that persecute Christians. It is known by the very general name Disciple-Making Movements. This is not the place to describe this work of God, but you can read about it many books. I think *Miraculous Movements* by Jerry Trousdale[77] is the most interesting.

A local pastor, my wife, and I will soon begin weekly training provided by Experience Life Church in Abilene, TX. Their senior pastor, Chris Galanos, wrote a book titled *From Megachurch to Multiplication*,[78] telling the story of their transition to the principles of disciple-making.

---

[77] 2012, Thomas Nelson
[78] 2018, Experience Life

This section in Disciple-Making Movements is irrelevant to *Rebuilding the Foundations*, but DMMs have documented tens of millions of people reached who are actively participating in hundreds of thousands of small churches around the world. I thought it was important to put you in touch with that kind of spiritual power. See https://www.experiencelifenow.com/wigtake-dmm-blog for contact.

"Now, brothers, I entrust you to God and to the word of his grace, which is able to build up, and to give you the inheritance among all those who are sanctified" (Acts 20:32).

Bibliography

ABC Memphis. (2021). "Evangelism Explosion Outline." Web. ABC Memphis – A Loving Church. Retrieved June 1, 2021 from https://abcmemphis.org/evangelism_explosion_outline

Ante-Nicene Fathers, The. (1885-1887). Translated and edited by Alexander Roberts and James Donaldson. 10 volumes. PDF. Reprint Grand Rapids, MI: Christian Literature Crusade, 2002. These can be read online at *http://earlychristianwritings.com* and *https://ccel.org/fathers.*

Anonymous. (c. 130-200). "Epistle to Diognetus." Translation from *The Ante-Nicene Fathers*: Vol. I

Apostolic Bible Polyglot Greek-English Interlinear. (n.d.). "1 Timothy 6:3-4." Web. Retrieved August 8, 2020 from https://studybible.info/interlinear/1%20Timothy%206:3-4

Athenagoras. (c. 175-180). *A Plea for the Christians*. Translation from *The Ante-Nicene Fathers*: Vol. II.

Barnabas (Pseudo-Barnabas). (c. 80-130). "Epistle of Barnabas." Translation from *The Ante-Nicene Fathers*: Vol. I.

Bercot, D. (1989). *Will the Real Heretics Please Stand Up*. Paperback. Scroll Publishing.

Berean Christian Bible Study Resources, 2009, "The Tenses." Web. Berean Christian Bible Study Resources. Retrieved June 15, 2020 from http://www.bcbsr.com/greek/gtense.html

BibleHub. (2004-2020). "1 John 3:9." Web. Retrieved August 4, 2020 from https://biblehub.com/commentaries/1_john/3-9.htm

Bible Study Tools. (2018). "The Date of the Pastoral Epistles." Web. Retrieved June 27, 2018 from https://www.biblestudytools.com/history/joseph-barber-lightfoot-biblical-essays/the-date-of-the-pastoral-epistles.html

British Magazine and Monthly Register. (1842). "Wesley a High Churchman." *The British Magazine and Monthly Register of Ecclesiastical and Religious Information, Parochial History, and Documents Reflecting the State of the Poor, Progress of Education, &c, volume XXII.* London:T. Clerc Smith. 1842. pp.

274-5. Retrieved July 6, 2020 from
https://books.google.com/books?id=oag2AQAAMAAJ&pg

Catholic Church. (2012). *Catechism of the Catholic Church*. Retrieved August 12, 2020 from http://www.scborromeo.org/ccc/p1s2c2.htm

Chrysostom, J. (d. 407). "The Homilies of St. John Chrysostom on Paul's Epistles to the Romans." Translation from *The Nicene and Post-Nicene Fathers*, Series I, Vol. 11.

Clement of Rome. (81-96). "I Clement." Translation from *The Ante-Nicene Fathers*: Vol. I.

Encyclopedia Britannica, Editors of. (n.d.). "Docetism." Web. Britannica. Retrieved September 4, 2021 from https://www.britannica.com/topic/Docetism

Eusebius (of Caesarea). (323). *Church History*. Translation from *The Nicene and Post-Nicene Fathers*: Series 2, Vol. I.

Evangelism Explosion International. (2015). "Assurance." Web. Retrieved September 4, 2021 from https://evangelismexplosion.org/assurance/

Evangelism Explosion International. (2018). "History." Web. Retrieved June 22, 2018 from http://evangelismexplosion.org/about-us/history/

Felix, M. (c. 160-250). *The Octavius*. Translation from *The Ante-Nicene Fathers*: Vol. IV.

Free Dictionary, The. (2003-2021). Web. Farlex, inc. https://www.thefreedictionary.com

Galanos, C. (2018). *From Megachurch to Multiplication: A Church's Journey Toward Movement*. Experience Life.

Hermas. (c. 160). *The Pastor of Hermas*. Translation from *The Ante-Nicene Fathers*: Vol. II.

Huntington, J. & Elliott, L. (1966). *On the Edge of Nowhere*. New York: Crown Publishers.

Ignatius. (107 or 116). "Epistle to the Magnesians." Translation from *The Ante-Nicene Fathers*: Vol. I.

Irenaeus. (c. 185). *Against Heresies*. Translation from *The Ante-Nicene Fathers*: Vol. I.

Jacobson, R. (2017). *The Unchurching Comic Book*. Web. Retrieved August 8, 2020 from http://www.unchurching.com/comic

Jewish Virtual Library. (n.d.). "Jewish Concepts: Slavery." Web. Jewish Virtual Library. Retrieved August 4, 2020 from https://www.jewishvirtuallibrary.org/slavery-in-judaism

Jobes, K. H. (2001). *Invitation to the Septuagint*. Grand Rapids, MI: Baker. p. 26. Cited by Institute of Biblical Greek. (1997.) "Translate the Greek Old Testament – Septuagint (LXX) Online Texts." Web. Retrieved August 8, 2020 from https://biblicalgreek.org/translate/lxx/

Jubilee. (2020). Merriam-Webster.com. Retrieved August 4, 2020 from Jubilee, 2020, Merriam-Webster.com

Justin Martyr. (c. 155-165). *First Apology*. Translation from *The Ante-Nicene Fathers*: Vol. I.

Justin Martyr. (c. 155-165). *Dialogue with Trypho: a Jew*. Translation from *The Ante-Nicene Fathers*: Vol. I.

Keating, C. (n.d.). "Greek Verbs (Shorter Definitions)." Web. Resources for Learning New Testament Greek. Retrieved July 16, 2018 from https://www.ntgreek.org/learn_nt_greek/verbs1.htm

Keating, C. (n.d.). "Greek Verb Tenses (Intermediate Discussion)." Web. Retrieved July 12, 2021 from https://ntgreek.org/learn_nt_greek/inter-tense.htm

Kennedy, D. J. (1970). *Evangelism Explosion*. Tyndale House

Liddell, H. G. & Scott, R. (Authors); Jones, H.S. & McKenzie, R. (Eds.). (1940). *A Greek-English Lexicon*. Web. Perseus Digital Library. Retrieved July 30, 2021 from http://www.perseus.tufts.edu/hopper/text?doc=Perseus:text:1999.04.0057:entry=xa/risma

McClintock, J. & Strong, J. (editors). (1891). Cyclopaedia Biblical Theological Ecclesiastical Literature. Vol. II. New York: Harper Brothers. Cited by Osburn, 2019, "Calvinism."

MetaCamp. (2020). "MetaCamp." Web. Retrieved August 8, 2020 from https://metacamp.org/

Moore, T. (2007-2020). Kata Biblon Greek Septuagint and Wiki English Translation. Web. Kata Biblon. Retrieved July 16, 2020 from https://en.katabiblon.com/us/index.php?text=LXX

Moore, T. (2007-2021). " Πέτρος, -ου, ὁ." Web. Kata Biblon. Retrieved June 18, 2021 from https://lexicon.katabiblon.com/index.php?lemma= Πέτρος

Nicene and Post-Nicene Fathers, The. (1886-1900). Series 1 was edited by Philip Schaff, and Series II was edited by Philip Schaff & Henry Wace.

Nichols, S. (2016). "The State of Theology: Does Even the Smallest Sin Deserve Eternal Damnation?". Web. Ligonier Ministries. Retrieved June 1, 2021 from https://www.ligonier.org/blog/state-theology-does-sin-deserve-damnation/

Osburn, G. (2019). "Calvinism." Web. The Apostolic Doctrine. Retrieved June 1, 2019 from https://www.theapostolicdoctrine.com/calvinism/

Pavao, P. (2009-2020). "The Trinity." Web. Retrieved September 14, 2020 from https://www.christian-history.org/the-trinity.html

Pavao, P. (2009-2021). Quotes About Sacrifices. Web. Christian History for Everyman. Retrieved July 26, 2021 from https://www.christian-history.org/sacrifices-quotes.html

Pavao, P. (2014). *Decoding Nicea*. Selmer, TN: Greatest Stories Ever Told.

Pavao, P. (2019). *Rome's Audacious Claim: Should Every Christian Be Subject to the Pope?*. Paperback. Selmer, TN: Greatest Stories Ever Told.

Polycarp. (c. 110-140). "Epistle to the Philippians." Translation from *The Ante-Nicene Fathers*: Vol. I.

GreekLexicon.org. (2012-2018). "591: ἀποδίδωμι." Web. Scripture Systems ApS. Retrieved July 10, 2021 from https://greeklexicon.org/lexicon/strongs/591/

Sider, R. (2005). *The Scandal of the Evangelical Conscience: Why are Christians Living Just Like the Rest of the World?*. Kindle. Grand Rapids, MI: BakerBooks. p. 13

Southern Baptist Convention. (1982). "Continuing Witness Training." Manual. Home Mission Board of the Southern Baptist Convention

State of Theology, The. (2017). "The State of Theology." Web. Ligonier. Retrieved July 8, 2018 from https://thestateoftheology.com/

Steele, D.N. & Thomas, C.C. (1963). *The Five Points of Calvinism*. Presbyterian & Reformed Pub. Co., p. 61. Cited by Osburn, 2019. "Calvinism"

Stegall, T. (2019). "Clarifying the Misunderstood Present Tense." Web. Grace Gospel Press. Retrieved July 26, 2020 from https://www.gracegospelpress.org/clarifying-the-misunderstood-present-tense/

Strauss, M. 2020. "John: The Gospel of the Eternal Son Who Reveals the Father." Web. The Bible Project. Retrieved June 15, 2020 from https://bibleproject.com/blog/john-gospel-eternal-son-reveals-father/

StudyBible.info. (n.d.). "G3084 λυτρόω - Strong's Greek Lexicon Number." Web. Retrieved August 28, 2021 from https://studybible.info/strongs/G3084

StudyBible.info. (n.d.). " G3085 λύτρωσις - Strong's Greek Lexicon Number." Web. Retrieved August 28, 2021 from https://studybible.info/strongs/G3085

StudyBible.info. (n.d.). "G3352 νοσέω – Strong's Greek Lexicon Number." Web. Retrieved August 8, 2020 from https://studybible.info/strongs/G3552

StudyBible.info. (n.d.). "G5486 χάρισμα - Strong's Greek Lexicon Number." Web. Retrieved July 10, 2021 from https://studybible.info/strongs/G5486

Tertullian. (c. 197-220). *Apology*. Translation from *The Ante-Nicene Fathers*: Vol. III.

Tertullian. (c. 197-220). *The Prescription Against Heretics*. Translation from *The Ante-Nicene Fathers*: Vol. III.

Trousdale, J. (1972). *Miraculous Movements: How Hundreds of Thousands of Muslims Are Falling in Love with Jesus*. Thomas Nelson.

Twain, Mark. (1906). letter to Charlotte Teller. Cited by Schmidt, B. (1997-2020). "Custom." Web. Mark Twain Quotations, Newspaper Collections, & Related Resources. Cited from Paine, A.B. (2008). *Mark Twain, A Biography: The Personal and Literary Life of Samuel Langhorne Clemens*. 2008 Edition. Kolthoff Press. Originally published 1912. p. 1285. Retrieved July 13, 2020 from http://www.twainquotes.com/Custom.html

Paul Pavao and Greatest Stories Ever Told®

Paul Pavao has published five other books through Greatest Stories Ever Told®:

- *Decoding Nicea* is the story of the Council of Nicea[79] that convened in A.D. 325 to settle a dispute over whether Jesus, the Son of God, was "begotten" [i.e., "born"] or "created" before all things. I tell the story from sources that precede or are contemporary to the council. Several graduates have told me they wished *Decoding Nicea* had been their textbook on the Trinity in Bible School.
- *Rome's Audacious Claim* is a careful refutation of the Roman Catholic claim that the pope has "full, supreme, and universal power over the whole Church" (*Catechism of the Catholic Church*, par. 882). The book uses original sources to describe and detail the rise of the bishop of Rome to widespread power. At the same time, I refute the claims of Roman Catholic Apologists like Jimmy Akin (*The Fathers Know Best*). Stephen Ray (*Upon This Rock*), and Scott Hahn (*Rome Sweet Home*).
- *The Apostles' Gospel* is a simple overview of the Gospel as preached by the apostles in the Book of Acts.
- *Grace: The Power of God and Promise of the New Testament* is a definition and description of grace from the New Testament Scriptures. It exposes the misuse of the word "grace" among evangelicals.

Greatest Stories Ever Told® has also published:

- *Forgotten Gospel: The Original Message of a Conquering King* by Matthew Bryan. *Forgotten Gospel* solidly and precisely lay out the Gospel of the Kingdom from both the Gospels and Old Testament prophecy.
- *Slavery During the Revolutionary War* by Esther Pavao not only covers slavery among the founding fathers, but lets the fathers and several slaves themselves describe the practice of slavery in the late 1700s.
- *The Promise* by Megan Rebekah Cupit is the Nativity Story from Mary's perspective. It brought tears to eyes at several

---

[79] or "Nicaea"

points. Just as "The Chosen" puts emotion and a real-life touch to the Gospels, Megan puts a real-life feel in the life of Mary and her divine child.

Paul Pavao also has two web sites and two blogs.

- Christian-history.org is "Christian History for Everyman." It focuses on early Christian history, the fourth century and the First Council of Nicea, and the Protestant Reformation.
- RebuildingtheFoundations.org contains my exhortations and theological articles, many of them pulled from my Ancient-Faith.com blog.
- Ancient-Faith.com is where I blog the things I am learning from God as I walk with him.
- Apostles-vs-Calvinism.org is where I blog topics related to this book.

Feel free to contact Paul at paul@christian-history.org or to friend him on Facebook. Feedback on the book is especially welcome. Your suggestions will help the book be updated on an ongoing basis.

www.ingramcontent.com/pod-product-compliance
Lightning Source LLC
Chambersburg PA
CBHW012207090526
44583CB00022BA/2940